BANJO HANDBOOK

By Janet Davis

Online Audio   www.melbay.com/94206BCDEB

Audio Contents

1	Bridge Positioning (pg. 8) [:30]
2	Roll Patterns (pg. 28) [:30]
3	Common Variations (pg. 29) [:47]
4	Advanced Patterns (pg. 29) [:46]
5	Bile 'em Cabbage Down–Forward Roll (pg. 30) [:25]
6	–Combining Different Rolls, Ex. 1 (pg. 30) [:22]
7	–Combining Different Rolls, Ex. 2 (pg. 30) [:23]
8	–Adding L. H. Techniques (pg. 31) [:26]
9	–L. H. Tech. & Varying the Rhythm (pg. 31) [:25]
10	The Gray Goose (pg. 32) [:34]
11	Goodnight Ladies (pg. 32) [:21]
12	Old MacDonald Had a Farm (pg. 32) [:37]
13	Do Lord, Oh Do Lord (pg. 33) [:37]
14	May I Sleep in Your Barn Tonight, Mister? (pg. 33) [:38]
15	Bully of the Town (pg. 34) [1:23]
16	Intros (pg. 35) [:50]
17	G Chord Licks (pg. 36) [:44]
18	C Chord Licks–1 & 2 Measure (pg. 37) [1:05]
19	D Chord Licks–1 & 2 Measure (pg. 38) [1:04]
20	A Chord Licks (pg. 39) [:28]
21	F, B, & E Chord Licks (pg. 40) [:46]
22	Little Maggie & Variations (pg. 41) [:43]
23	Cripple Creek (pg. 42) [:24]
24	Cumberland Gap & Wildwood Flower (pg. 42) [:41]
25	Mama Don't Allow (pg. 43) [:25]
26	Wreck of the Old '97 (pg. 43) [:27]
27	Intros–Up the Neck–G & C Chords (pg. 46) [:48]
28	G Chord Licks (pg. 47) [:30]
29	C Chord Licks (pg. 48) [:25]
30	D Chord Licks (pg. 48) [:25]
31	A & F Chord Licks (pg. 49) [:29]
32	B & E Chord Licks (pg. 49) [:36]
33	Bile 'em Cabbage Down & Variation (pg. 50) [:36]
34	Cumberland Gap (pg. 50) [:18]
35	Little Maggie & Variation (pg. 51) [:34]
36	Wreck of the Old '97 (pg. 51) [:28]
37	Mama Don't Allow (pg. 52) [:32]
38	She'll Be Coming Around the Mountain (pg. 52) [:28]
39	Dixie (pg. 54) [:23]
40	Scale Patterns (pg. 55) [:14]
41	Circular Scale (pg. 56) [:17]
42	G & C Chord Licks (pg. 56) [:40]
43	D, A & F Chord Licks (pg. 56) [:26]
44	Cripple Creek (pg. 57) [:29]
45	Blackberry Blossom (pg. 57) [:54]
46	Fire on the Mountain (pg. 58) [:51]
47	Red Haired Boy (pg. 58) [:48]
48	The Dusty Miller (pg. 59) [:43]
49	Vamping Patterns 1-6 (pg. 62) [1:01]
50	Back Up Licks 1-5 (pg. 63) [:59]
51	Back Up Licks 6-12 (pg. 64) [1:34]
52	Back Up Licks 13-19 (pg. 65) [1:31]
53	Back Up Licks 20-22 (pg. 66) [1:18]
54	Bile 'em Cabbage Down & Variations (pg. 67) [1:04]
55	May I Sleep in Your Barn Tonight, Mister? (pg. 68) [:38]
56	She'll Be Coming Around the Mountain (pg. 68) [:39]
57	Mama Don't Allow (pg. 69) [:32]
58	Wreck of the Old '97 (pg. 69) [:41]
59	Song Endings: Parts A & B (pg. 70) [:54]
60	Just Because (pg. 73) [:45]
61	Fisher's Hornpipe–Key of G (pg. 74) [:49]
62	Fisher's Hornpipe–Key of D (pg. 74) [:43]
63	Soldier's Joy (pg. 78) [:58]
64	John Henry (pg. 78) [:33]
65	Reuben (pg. 79) [1:43]
66	Bile 'em Cabbage–D Tuning (pg. 79) [:30]
67	Bile 'em Cabbage–Intro (pg. 80) [:49]
68	Bile 'em Cabbage–Song & Variation [:50]

Cover photo courtesy of Liberty Banjo Company, Bridgeport, Connecticut.

1 2 3 4 5 6 7 8 9 0

Visit us on the Web at www.melbay.com — E-mail us at email@melbay.com

Table Of Contents

This section explains the features of the banjo as an instrument, and suggests possible ways to achieve the best sound.

This sections discusses the basic tools necessary for playing in the 3 - finger style.

This section covers the chord positions used by the left hand, and provides complete Chord Charts.

This section provides the building blocks for playing any song on the banjo in Scruggs - style.

This sections discusses playing in the 5th - 22nd fret area of the fingerboard, (higher pitches).

This section covers playing in the "Melodic", or "Fiddle" Style of 3 - finger picking.

This section covers methods for playing accompaniment.

Covers possible ways to end a song in the Key of G.

This section is concerned with playing any song in any key, and the possible methods involved.

NOTE: Each section is followed by songs which demonstrate the techniques covered by the section.

Introduction

This handbook is intended for use as a reference manual for 5-string banjo players who are interested in the 3-finger style of playing.

It is designed to give you a quick explanation of the proper and/or most common methods for setting up the banjo and for playing the banjo.

The handbook is divided into nine main sections. Each section will begin with a brief introduction and a "how to" discussion, followed by examples of songs demonstrating the specific techniques discussed in the section.

Hopefully you will find useful information in each section of this book. Remember, an important part of playing the banjo, is learning about it, and enjoying it!

NOTES:————————————————————————————————————
1.) For more information on the techniques involved in working out and being able to play any song on the banjo, refer to:
SPLITTING THE LICKS by Janet Davis (Mel Bay Publication).
2.) For more information on playing back up, refer to:
BACK UP BANJO by Janet Davis (Mel Bay Publication).

The Banjo Set Up

To achieve the ultimate sound from your banjo, you should experiment with the set up, until you are satisfied. Generally, the rule is that "tighter" results in a crisper sound.

IN THIS SECTION:

Setting the bridge

The Head

The Tailpiece

The Strings

The Action

The Truss Rod

NOTES:______________________________________

Periodically, you should check <u>all</u> of the parts, including screws, bracket hooks, etc. to make certain that they are tight. Vibration from playing will cause these to loosen.

The Banjo And Its Parts

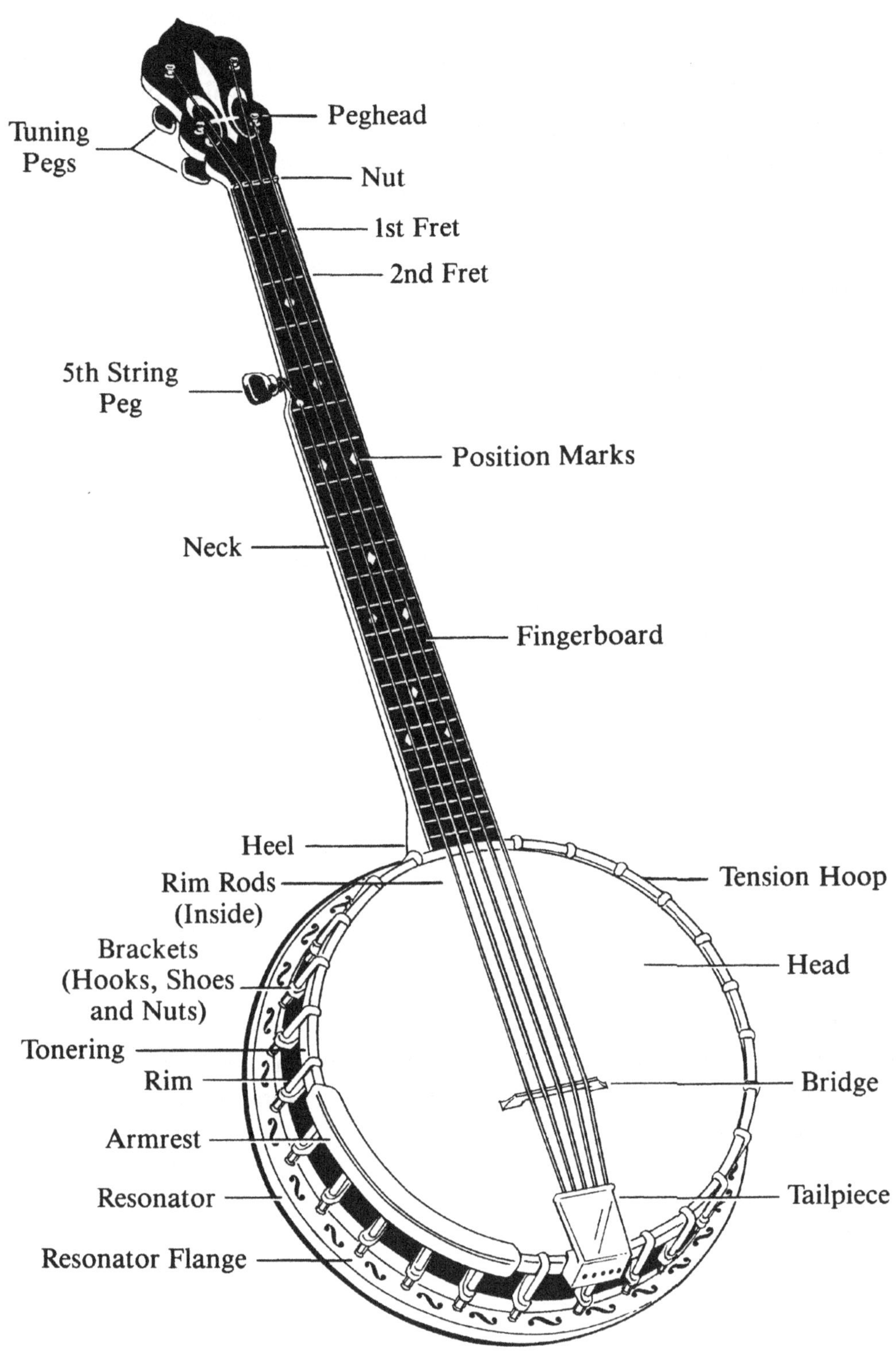

The Bridge

TYPE OF BRIDGE The type of bridge, (i.e. material, shape, size), is very influential over the tone produced from the banjo.

Popular types of bridges are:
1. 5/8" maple/ebony--standard for 3-finger style of playing.
2. 11/16" maple/ebony, often with wider spacing between strings--used by many professionals for more volume and purer tone.
3. 1/2" maple/ebony--popular for frailing & clawhammer. May cause buzzing in some banjos.
4. Compensated 5/8" or 1/2"--corrects pitch problems inherent in the banjo--esp. on 3rd string.

NOTES:
1. Each of the above types is a 3-footed bridge.
2. People occasionally thin the bridge with sandpaper, in order to achieve a brighter tone. However, this may also lengthen the sustain of the tones.
3. A bridge can be made from just about any material, although the maple body with an ebony top is standard.

The Bridge

PLACING THE BRIDGE

Setting the bridge in the proper position is critical for accurate pitch.

1. Measure the distance along the 2nd & 3rd strings, from the nut to the front of the 12th fretbar, (app. 13¼").
2. Place the bridge on the head, exactly the same distance found in step 1, from the back (bridge's) side of the 12th fretbar.
3. Center the bridge on the head, so that the 3rd string runs along the middle of the fingerboard at the 19th fret.
4. Tune the banjo.

CHECKING THE PLACEMENT

Play the following:

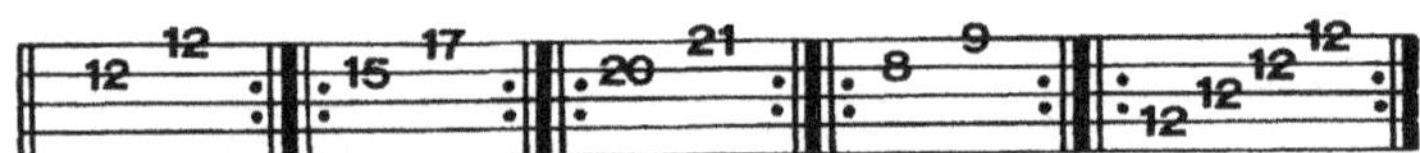

The tones should ring in pure harmony. If, as you move up the neck, the notes sound out of tune:

1. Flat (too low): move the bridge back, toward the tailpiece.
2. Sharp (too high): move the bridge up, toward the fingerboard.

NOTES: ____
1. Loosen the strings before setting the bridge.
2. The 12th fretbar is the midpoint between the nut and bridge.
3. Measure from the fingerboard side of the nut, and the fingerboard side of the bridge.

The Head

TYPE OF HEAD

Standard is an 11 inch head of plastic (mylar) material. High crown is specified for a flathead ring; Low crown is specified for an archtop ring.

The type of head, (material, coating, thickness, & tightness) will affect the sound of your banjo.

Popular types are:

1. White Frosted -- probably most common
2. White Smooth -- thinner, crisper tone
3. Clear -- aesthetically nice; crisp tone
4. Waverly Fiberskyn -- simulated calfskin; warm tone.

TIGHTENING THE HEAD

Tighten the head to increase crispness of tone. However, too tight results in breakage, and/or loss of tone.

1. Remove resonator.
2. With bracket wrench, tighten (½ turn), each bracket nut. Go around the rim several times. (Some recommend that you work diagonally.)
3. Keep the tension hoop level.
4. Squeaks signal the warning that the head should be about tight enough.
5. Some people tap the head, until they hear a specific tone, (usually A or B); dampen the strings so they don't vibrate.

NOTES:

1. The standard size is 11" across the diameter of the head. Odd sizes are available, also.
2. Prewar banjo heads were originally of calfskin, which were very weather sensitive. Most people prefer the mylar heads of today.

The Tailpiece

When choosing a tailpiece, there are several possible considerations. What is its metallic content? Is it cast or stamped? Long or short? Adjustable? Compensated, or are the holes in a straight line?

METAL Some feel that a brass tailpiece produces the purest tone.

CAST A cast tailpiece is generally more expensive.

LENGTH A longer tailpiece may produce a stronger tone, with more bass. A shorter tailpiece may produce a crisper tone.

TENSION If adjustable, the tighter the tailpiece is, (the closer it is to the head), the brighter and crisper the sound. However, too tight may choke the sound.

A less tight tailpiece produces a more open tone which may bring out the bass.

Some professionals keep the tailpiece just tight enough so that it doesn't rattle, or fall off the banjo, for a more open sound.

COMPENSA-TION With a compensated tailpiece, the hole for the third string (middle hole) is set back so that the third string is longer than the others, to compensate for the tendency of this string to sharp, especially at the 4th and 12th frets.

TYPES Popular choices are the Kerschner, the Presto, the Waverly, and the Clamshell.

NOTES:____

1.) Experimentation is the key to setting up a banjo.

The Strings

CHOOSING STRINGS

Strings are usually chosen by brand and by gauge (thickness). The type of steel may also be a consideration.

<u>Light</u> <u>gauge</u> have less tension, and require a slightly lighter playing touch, in order to avoid buzzing.

<u>Medium</u> <u>gauge</u> require a slightly stronger playing touch, and have less tendency to buzz with a low action.

CHANGING THE STRINGS

Change the strings one at a time.
(Do not remove all five at once.)

1. Thread the new string through the proper hole in the tailpiece. (Hook the loop on the proper hook.)
2. Then, thread the opposite end through the hole in the string post for the corresponding tuning peg.
3. Wind the peg toward the outside of the peghead, holding the string so that it doesn't slip.
4. As the string becomes tight, place it in the correct slot in the nut & bridge.
5. Caution: don't wind it too tightly, past the correct pitch point, or it will break.

NOTES: ____

1. You can pull several inches of the string through the tuning peg, and clip the excess with a wire cutter, if you prefer.
2. Strings should be changed about once a month to keep a responsive tone.
3. A phosphor bronze 4th string produces a brighter tone, but does not last as long.
4. Each person must experiment to find his preference.
5. The same type of strings may feel different on each banjo.

The Action

THE ACTION   The action is the distance of the strings to the fingerboard.

A high action results in more volume, and tone clarity; left-hand techniques may be easier to execute, (hammers, etc.)

A low action results in easier lefthand fingering. Also, it may help speed playing.

ADJUSTING THE ACTION: i.e for buzzing, more volume, easier playing, etc. Remember!!! A little goes a long way!

THE COORDINATOR RODS: Coordinator rods can be used to raise or lower the action. (Be careful.)

1. Remove resonator.
2. If your banjo has two rods inside, the upper rod is only for support.
3. Loosen nut on upper rod.
4. Place nail through hole in lower rod; hold this rod in place; do not turn it. Do not let this rod slip, while turning the nuts to adjust the action.
5. Using a ½ inch open end wrench to adjust the neck angle:

    LOWER THE ACTION: Loosen (slightly) the nut inside the rim. Tighten the nut outside the rim (slightly).

    RAISE THE ACTION: loosen (slightly) the nut outside the rim. Then, slightly tighten the nut inside the rim.

6. Retighten the nut on the upper rod.

NOTES: ____
1. Overtightening can result in breaking the rim! Be careful!
2. ¼ of a turn is a lot!

The Truss Rod

Most professional banjos have an adjustable truss rod, which runs from the peghead, through the neck and into the heel of the banjo, to prevent the neck from warping, and to correct possible warpage if it does occur, by allowing you to alter the curve of the fingerboard. It can also be used to adjust the action in this manner. Use care and patience, however, for you can ruin your neck.

TO CHECK FOR WARPAGE

Place a straight edge along your fingerboard, over the frets. According to most luthiers, there should be no more than a 1/32" clearance at the 12th fret, when holding down a string at the 1st and 22nd frets.   If the clearance is greater, the neck may need adjusting.

TO CHECK THE ACTION

Many banjo players prefer a slight curve (warp) in the fingerboard, for a quicker, more responsive banjo. To achieve this, there should be no more than a 1/64" to 1/32" clearance from the top of the 7th fret bar to the bottom of the string, when holding down a string at the 1st and 22nd frets. (Run a spare 4th string across the 7th fret bar, under the strings. It should barely fit.)

ADJUSTING THE TRUSS ROD

1.) Remove the cover plate

2.) With a hex wrench or an Allen Wrench, turn the nut 1/4". Check with straight edge. Clockwise to tighten—will straighten the neck from: _______ to _______ .

Counterclockwise to loosen—will slightly warp the neck from: ___ to ___, (or will straighten the neck from too much bow, ___ to ___).

Playing Basics

This section provides the basic tools for playing any song on the 5-string banjo in the 3-finger style of playing. The items in this section are particularly helpful for beginners, but are used by almost every banjo player.

IN THIS SECTION:

Holding the Banjo

Fingerpicks

Tuning the Banjo
-- G Tuning --

Tablature & Rhythm

Left Hand Techniques

NOTES:____
1.) For additional basics for playing any song on the banjo, refer to the section on Common Chord Positions, and to the section on Right Hand Roll Patterns.

HOW TO HOLD THE BANJO

1. Sit up straight.

2. Do NOT lay the banjo flat on its back in your lap.

3. The peghead should be about level with your left shoulder.

4. A strap (preferably **all** leather), will aid in holding the banjo securely.

5. Your left hand holds the neck, your right hand plucks the strings over the drum.

6. Comfort is **important.**

HOW TO WEAR FINGERPICKS

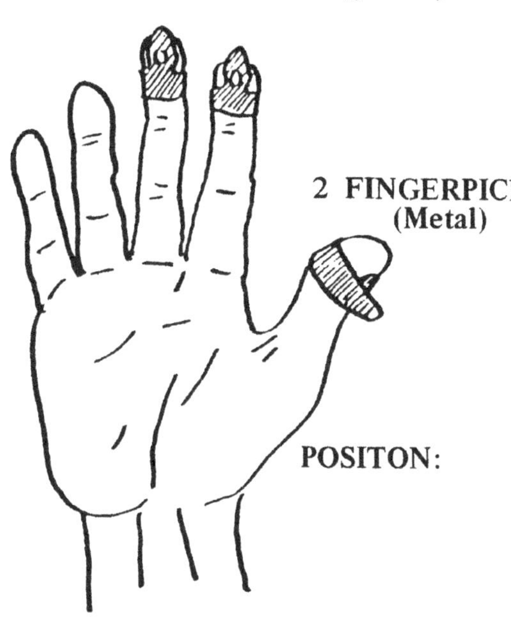

THUMBPICK:
(plastic)

wear it in the traditional way, with the curve around the fingernail side of the thumb.   Often thumbpicks don't fit snugly. Reshape it by holding it in hot water & molding it. It should fit tight enough so it doesn't slip around.

2 FINGERPICKS:
(Metal)

wear the curved part along the flesh side of your finger, not the fingernail side. Wear one pick on your Index finger & one on your Middle finger (right-hand).   Bend the picks to fit snugly. The picks should extend about 1/8 inch from the tips of your fingers. *

POSITON:

place picks on your fingers so they pick the strings on the flat side . . . NOT at an angle. (If at an angle, they will squeak on the strings.) Keep the Thumb straight when it picks. Pick with short strokes.   Thumb plucks down, fingers pluck up.

NOTES: ______________________________________

*1.   Picks are a personal choice. Shorter points may provide easier playing, but longer points provide a crisper tone. (Some people even wrap the fingerpick flush around the tip of their finger **for more power.)**

Tuning The Banjo
G TUNING

G TUNING
G D G B D

This is the most common tuning used for three--finger picking.

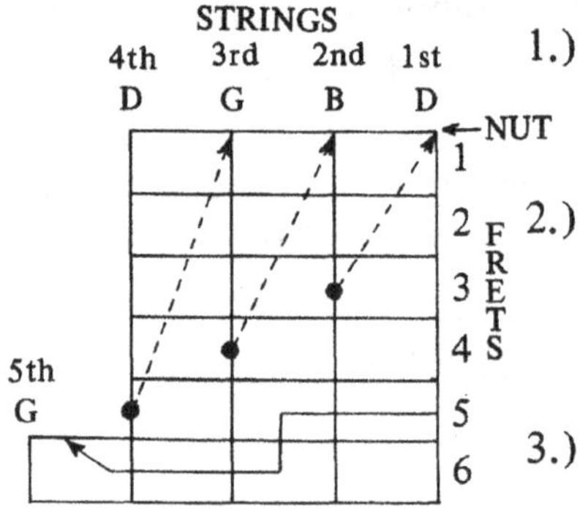

1.) Tune the 4th string to a **D**. (D below middle C on the piano). This is the deepest pitch on the banjo.

2.) Depress the 4th string at the 5th fret, and tune the 3rd string to this pitch, (<u>G</u> below middle C). (The open 3rd string sounds like the 4th string fretted at the 5th fret.)

3.) Depress the 3rd string at the 4th fret and tune the 2nd string to this pitch, (<u>B</u> below middle C). (The open 2nd string sounds like the 3rd string fretted at the 4th fret.)

4.) Hold the 2nd string on the 3rd fret and tune the 1st string to this pitch, (<u>D</u> next to middle C on the piano). (The open 1st string sounds like the 2nd string fretted on the 3rd fret.)

5.) Depress the 1st string at the 5th fret, and tune the 5th string to this pitch. (<u>G</u> above middle C). The open 5th string sounds like the 1st string, 5th fret.)

6.) When tuned correctly, the strings will sound a G chord, when strummed.

NOTES:
1.) A piano or a pitchpipe will help.
2.) Electronic tuners are also now available, which are easy to use, and automatically tell you when each string is in tune.
3.) G Tuning notation:

If you have a piano:

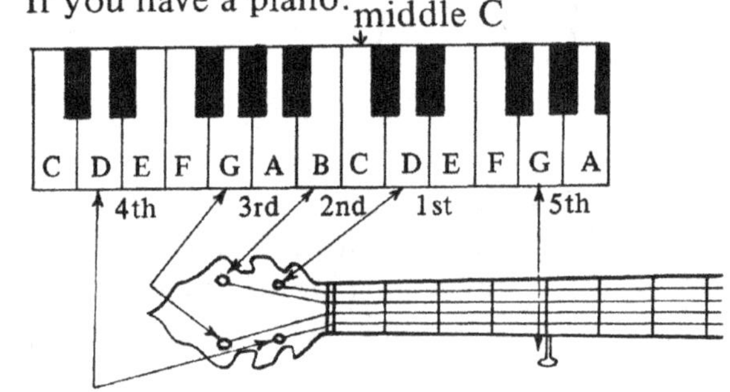

Tablature

PURPOSE Tablature is designed for those who do not read music. It can be learned in a few minutes.

DEFINITION The lines tell you which string to pick; the numbers tell you which fret number to hold (on that string) with the left hand.

the lines are the five strings.

the numbers are fret numbers, (4th fret.)

Two numbers, one over the other, are to be played at the same time; this is called a pinch.

RHYTHM The duration, or length of time, each note should ring, is indicated by the stem, (line drawn from each number.) (Some notes receive different counts than others; they will use different stems.)

=quarter note. (Hold for the duration of two eighth notes.)

=eighth note. (Play two eighth notes or one quarter note for the same duration.

=sixteenth note. (Play two sixteenth notes for the duration of one eighth note; play four sixteenth notes for the duration of one quarter note.)

NOTES:____

1.) Many books contain more detail on reading rhythm.

Left Hand Techniques

Often the "fancy" embellishments played in an arrangement on the banjo involve sounding the notes with the left hand.

PROCEDURE — The right hand picks the note that occurs just in front of the LH Technique; then the left hand executes the specified technique, in order to sound the specified tone.

TYPES — Each of the following is performed by the left hand, after a note is picked by the right hand:

H = Hammer: — the left finger literally "hammers" the indicated fret, in order to sound the tone. (Press hard with the left finger.)

P = Pull Off: — the left finger plucks the string, after fretting it on the indicated fret, in order to make it sound.

SL = Slide: — The left finger slides from the previous note to the note indicated with the SL, in order to sound the latter.

↑
CH = Choke: — The left finger bends the string, after it is picked, to raise the pitch.
↓
CH = Choke: — The left finger bends the string before it is picked, then straightens it to lower the pitch.

NOTES: ____
1.) The right hand may pick another note at the same time.

Chords

When playing the banjo, the left hand usually works from chord positions, while the right hand picks the strings. Chords can be played on the deepest tones of the banjo, where many of the strings are left open, (not fretted by the left hand).

Chords can also be played "up-the-neck using three basic chord positions patterns with the left hand, where every string is fretted with the left hand.

IN THIS SECTION:

Common Chord Positions

The Major Chord Patterns

Chord Charts
    Major Chords
    Minor Chords
    Augmented Chords
    Diminished Chords

Common Positions

CHORDS ARE IMPROTANT: In every song played on the banjo, the left hand works from chord positions, while the right hand picks the strings.

CHORD SYMBOLS: Chord symbols are located above the tablature. When you see a chord symbol above the tablature in a song, (i.e. C), you should hold that chord position with the left hand.

The following positions are the most commonly played chords in the open string area of the fingerboard, (1st - 5th fret):

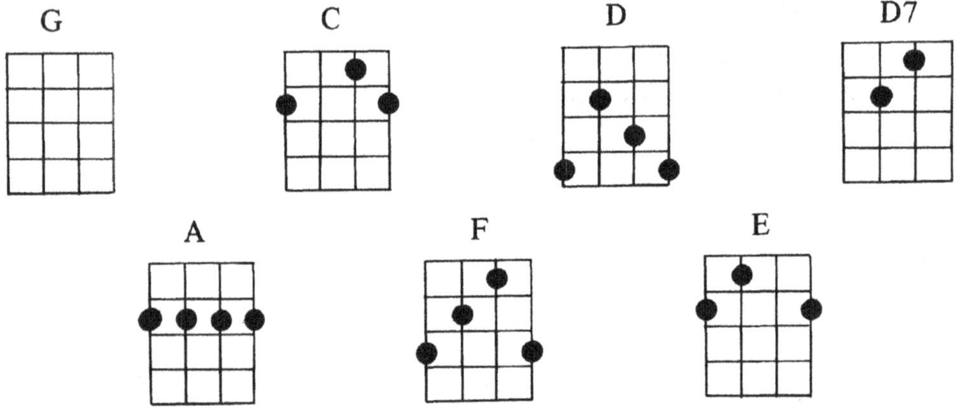

NOTES: ____
   1.) The G and D chords often work with open strings.
   2.) The most common chords played on the banjo are G, C, and D chords. A and F are also common.

The Major Chord Patterns

The following left hand patterns can be used to play any Major Chord.

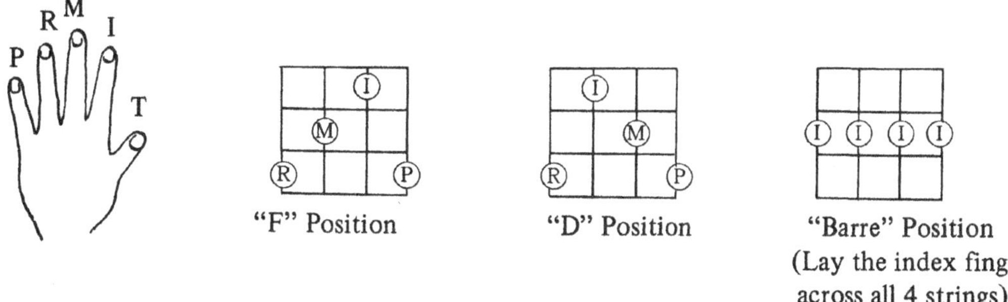

Each of the above patterns can be moved up the fingerboard to play any major chord. The chord names change in alphabetical order as each pattern travels up the neck.

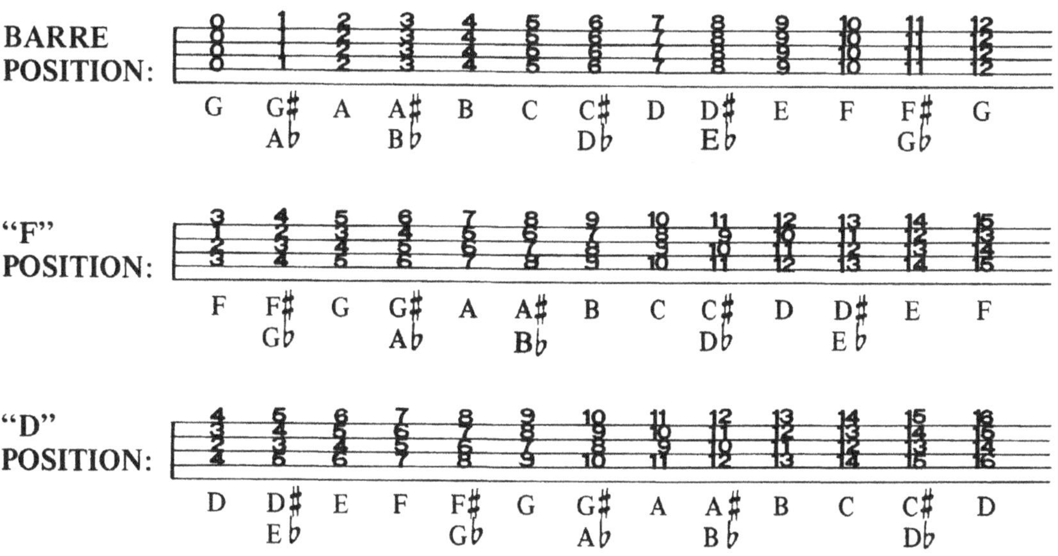

NOTES:

1.) All of the other chords, i.e. minor, diminished, augmented, etc. can be found in relation to these three positions.

2.) Be careful to use the correct left hand fingers to form each chord position, for licks work from these positions.

Chord Chart–G Tuning
MAJOR CHORDS

Major chords are formed from the 1st, 3rd, & 5th tones of the major scale of the chord name. There are three left hand positions for all of the major chords. (see p. 21)

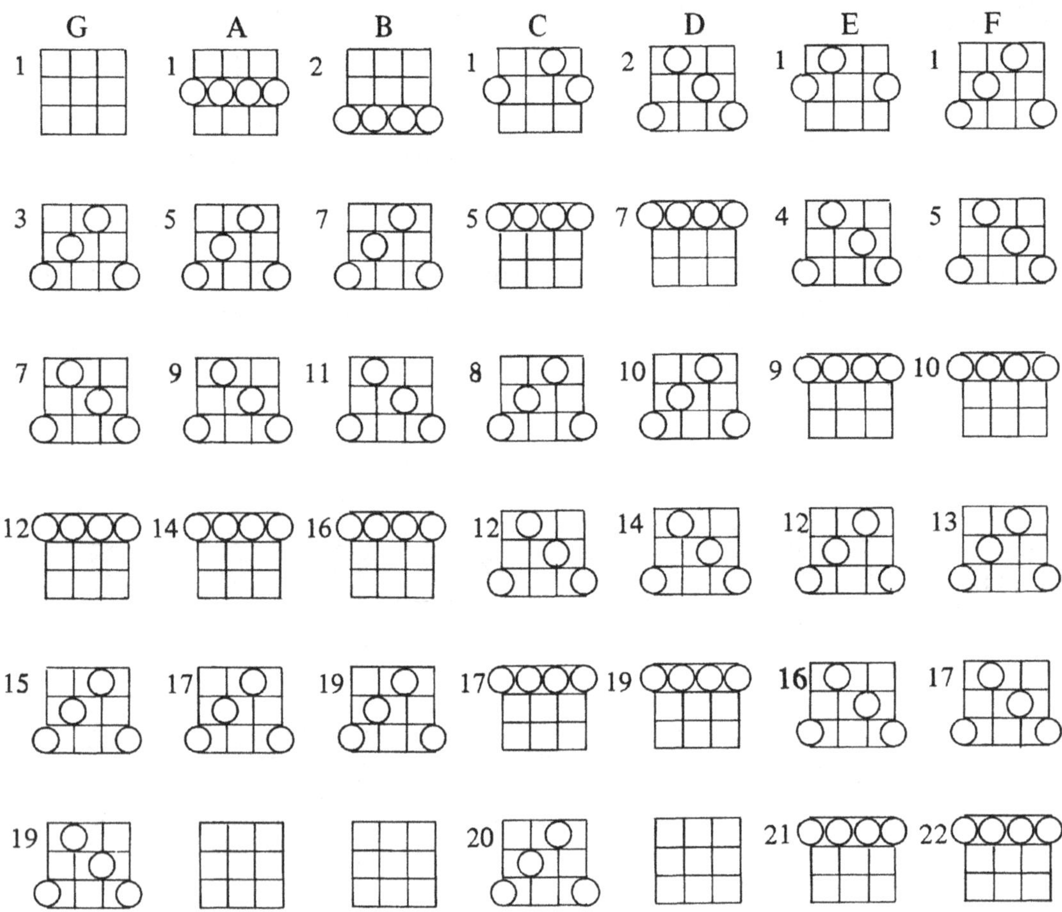

The number by each individual diagram tells you what fret the chord starts on.
(For ♯ & ♭ chords, see p.21.)

NOTES FOR THE ADVANCED PLAYER: ________________

Major chords provide the primary chords for songs played in major keys. (Most bluegrass songs fall into this category.) In addition, they can also be substituted for other chords in a song, either to fulfill the function of that chord, or to add color to the back-up. For example, a major chord can:

1.) Be used as a lower neighbor chord for color, (play the chord 2 (or 1) frets lower than the chord it is being substituted for). i.e. for G, play F, (or G-F-G).

2.) Be used as a passing chord to lead the music from one chord to another.

3.) Be substituted for its relative minor (or its secondary minor), (for a minor chord 2 letters before (or after) the chord name in the alphabet--i.e. G for em: C for am: D for bm.)

4.) Substitute as the ♭V chord of any chord--i.e. substitute A♭ for D: D♭ for G: (This works nicely for a V-I progression--i.e. instead of playing D to G, play A♭ (for D) to G.)

Minor Chords
(SYMBOL-m)

A minor chord is formed by flatting the 3rd of the major chord of the same name. There are three left hand positions for all of the minor chords.

The number by each individual diagram tells you what fret the chord starts on. (Minor chords are usually indicated with small letters.)

NOTES:

Minor chords are frequently used in back-up as substitute chords. For example:

1. Substitute a minor chord for its relative major chord. i.e. for G play em; for C play am; for D play bm. This adds color to the back-up.
2. Substitute the secondary minor chord for its major chord. i.e. for G play bm; for C play em; for D play f♯m. (The minor chord located a major 3rd higher.)
3. Substitute the parallel minor for its major chord in a IV-I progression. i.e. for C to G, play cm to G, (or C-cm-G); for G-D, play gm-D.
4. Substitute the minor ii chord for the major V chord. i.e. for V-I play ii-I, for D to G, play am to G instead; for G to C play dm to C instead.
5. Minor chords are often used as passing chords. i.e. for a V-I chord change, play V-IV-iii-ii I. (The first four chords are played for the V chord.) For ex. play D-C-bm-am (for D) then G; play G-F-em-dm-to go to C. Also: as passing chords for I-IV substitute III-♭III-II-(for I)-then play IV. i.e. to go from G to C play em-e♭m-dm (for G) then C. (Many times in the key of G, the link between a verse & chorus can use this. Also: for I-IV you can play I-ii-iii- IV. (i.e. G am-bm- C, for G to C)

Augmented Chords
(SYMBOL =+)

An augmented chord is formed by raising the 5th of the major chord of the same name. The left hand fingering position is the <u>same</u> for all augmented chords.

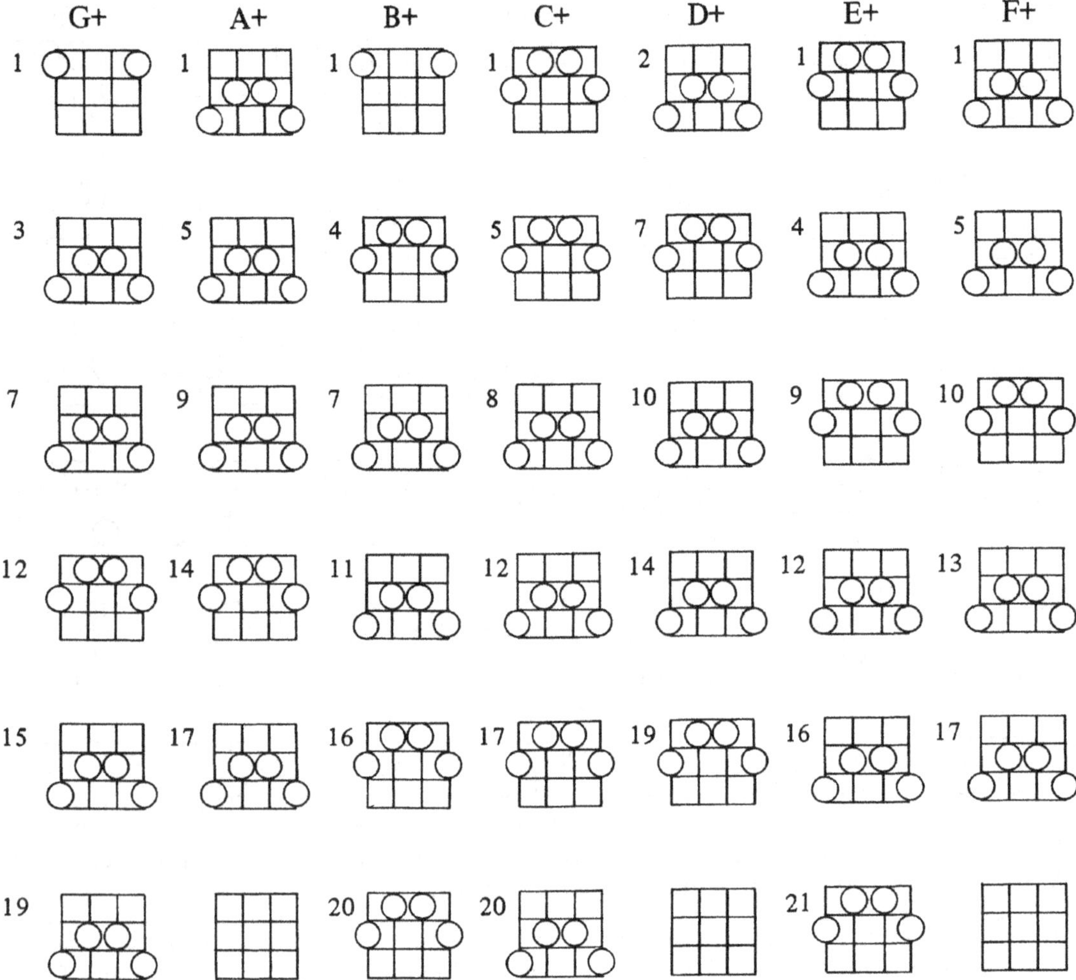

The number by each individual diagram indicates the fret the chord starts on.

NOTES: ____

Augmented chords are frequently used as substitute chords to lead the ear of the listener into a new chord. For example:

1. When going from the V chord back to the I chord. play the V+ chord instead of the major V chord. i.e. instead of playing D then G, play D+ then G.

2. Augment the I chord before going to the IV chord. i.e. in the Key of G, play G+ to go to C, rather than the regular (major) G chord.

3. Augmented chords are frequently substituted for 7th chords.

Diminished Chords
(SYMBOL=O)

The diminished chord is formed by flatting the 3rd and the 5th of the major chord. Although the diminished chord can be formed by the left hand in several different positions, more commonly, the $\flat$7th is added to the chord, so that <u>the same fingering position on the banjo can be used to play several diminished chords of different</u> names. The following are the most popular diminished chord positions. (Each position can be played three frets higher for the same chords.)

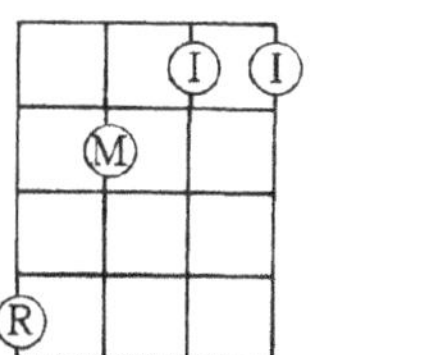

OR

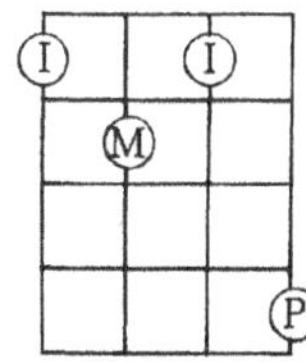

Barre the left index across all four strings

When the lowest tones of these positions are held on the:

*1st fret, the chord is f$\sharp$○, a○, c○, e$\flat$○, g$\flat$○, and d$\sharp$○. (Any of these.) The same position begun on any of the following frets will also result in the above chords: 4th, 7th, 10th, 13th, 16th, 19th.

  2nd fret, the chord is g○, b$\flat$○, d$\flat$○, f$\flat$○, e○, a$\sharp$○, and c$\sharp$○. The same position begun on any of the following frets will also result in the above chords: 5th, 8th, 11th, 14th, 17th, 20th.

  3rd fret, the chord is g$\sharp$○, b○, d○, f○, a$\flat$○, and c$\flat$○. These chords can also be played at the 6th, 9th, 12th, 15th, 18th, 21st fets.

NOTES: ____

All of the tones in a fully diminished 7th chord are located a minor 3rd apart. Due to the equidistance of the intervals, this chord can be resolved in four directions, (each tone leads to a different chord.) Because this chord is so unstable, it has many uses both for color and for function. For example:

1. As a passing chord–play the diminished position of the vii chord of the major chord you are changing to. i.e. play f$\sharp$○ then G; or C$\sharp$○ then D. (The passing chord is played while the song is on the chord you are changing from.)

2. As a substitute chord for V (substitute vii○ for V). i.e. substitute f$\sharp$○ for D; b○ for G. This is particularly useful when going from V-I. For example, for D to G, play f$\sharp$○ instead of D, then play the G chord.

3. In a IV to I progression, iv○ or i○ can be used as a passing chord. i.e. C to c○ to G instead of simply C to G; or C to g○ to G instead of simply C to G.

4. Diminished chords are useful as pivot chords to achieve quick modulations into remote keys.

Three-Finger Style Picking

This style of picking was popularized in the early 1940's by Earl Scruggs, Don Reno, and others, and continues to be a primary style of playing the 5-string banjo, today. It is often referred to as "Scruggs-style", for Earl Scruggs has done more to develop this style of playing than probably anyone else.

When playing in this style, the right Thumb, Index and Middle fingers pick the strings, while the ring finger and/or the little finger are braced on the head of the banjo for support.

IN THIS SECTION:

Right Hand Technique

Roll Patterns

Intros

Licks

Songs

Right Hand Technique

PICKING FINGERS

The thumb, index, and middle fingers of the right hand pick the strings of the banjo in the 3-finger style of playing. Generally, they will pick the strings in a specific order, forming picking patterns, called "rolls" or "licks".

FOR A CLEAR, CRISP TONE

Brace the little finger and/or the ring finger of the right hand on the head of the banjo, (in front of the bridge), for firm picking power.

Extend the fingerpicks about 1/8 inch from the tip of your fingers.

Pick the strings with short strokes, (staccato). Long strokes will run the tones together.

HAND POSITION

The "X" POSITION: (standard)
Pick near the bridge, especially when playing the deeper tones of the banjo. This produces a sharp, crisp tone.

The "Y" POSITION: (up-the-neck)
Pick near the fingerboard, away from the bridge, especially when playing on the higher fret numbers, (higher pitches). This produces a mellow tone.

NOTES:
1. Don't touch the bridge when bracing the little finger. This will stifle or dampen the tone.
2. Experiment with the fingerpicks.
3. Expression can be enhanced by varying your hand position.

Roll Patterns

Roll Patterns are the basis for all songs played in Scruggs-style on the banjo.
Each song is comprised of various combinations of rolls.

THE PATTERN: Each roll is a right hand picking pattern. Each roll is named
for the order or sequence in which the right hand fingers follow one another.

Any chord can be held with the left hand, while playing each
roll.

THE STANDARD BASIC ROLL PATTERNS

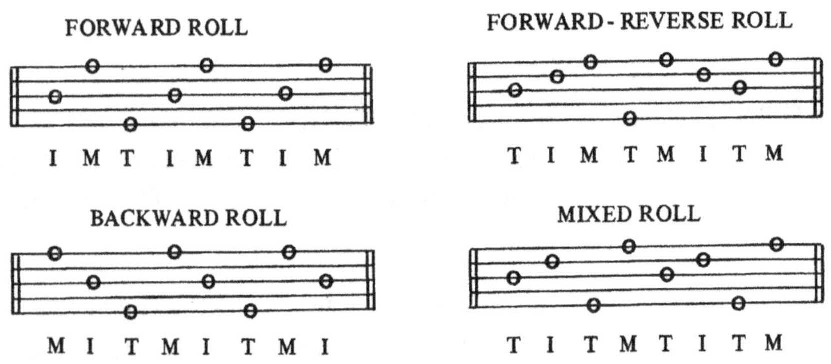

NOTES:
1.) Combine roll patterns according to the chords for the song.
2.) Generally, the beginning finger picks melody notes, while the other
two fingers play background, or harmony notes.
3.) Each roll pattern is played with 8 (eighth) notes, (one measure of
music or tablature).

COMMON VARIATIONS: Any roll pattern can be varied simply by changing the order in which the right fingers pick the strings.

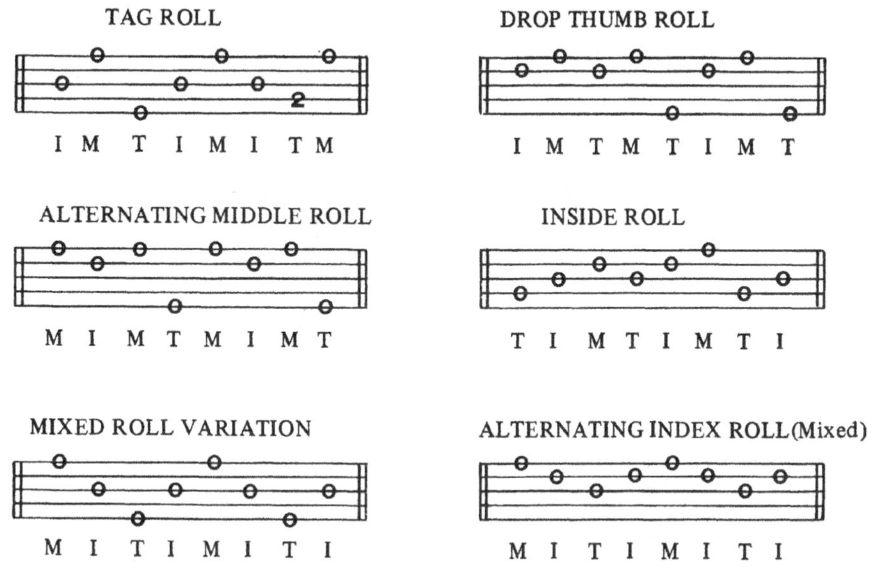

ADVANCED: These patterns are often found in the playing of contemporary professional banjo players.

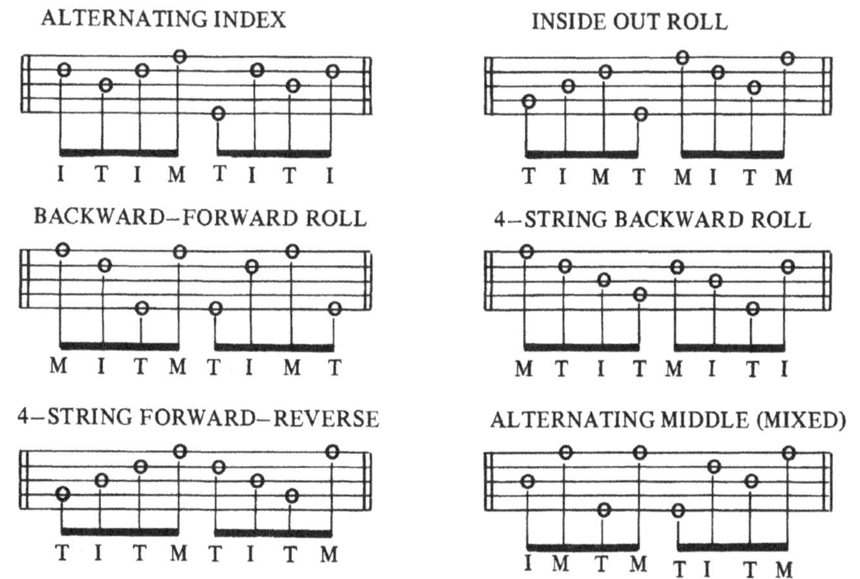

Using Roll Patterns

The following arrangement is built with rolls. Each measure in the following arrangement contains a roll pattern. The finger which begins each pattern picks the melody, while the other two fingers pick background or harmony notes (chords tones).

BILE 'EM CABBAGE DOWN
THE FORWARD ROLL

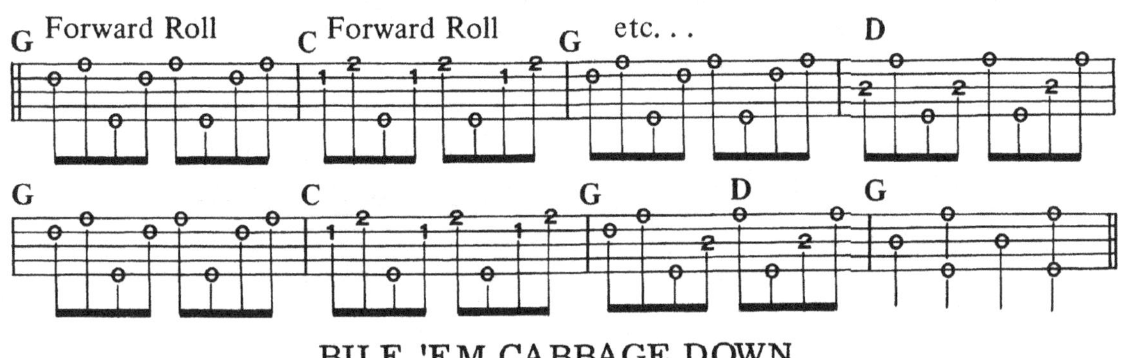

BILE 'EM CABBAGE DOWN
COMBINING DIFFERENT ROLLS

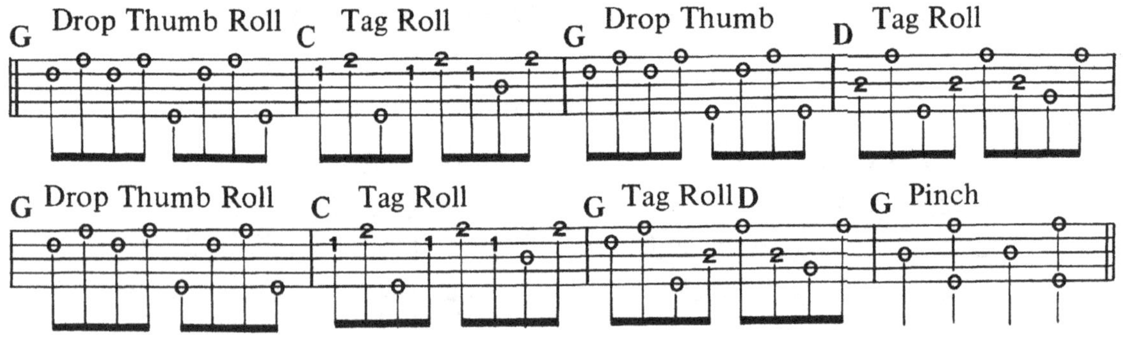

BILE 'EM CABBAGE DOWN
COMBINING DIFFERENT ROLLS

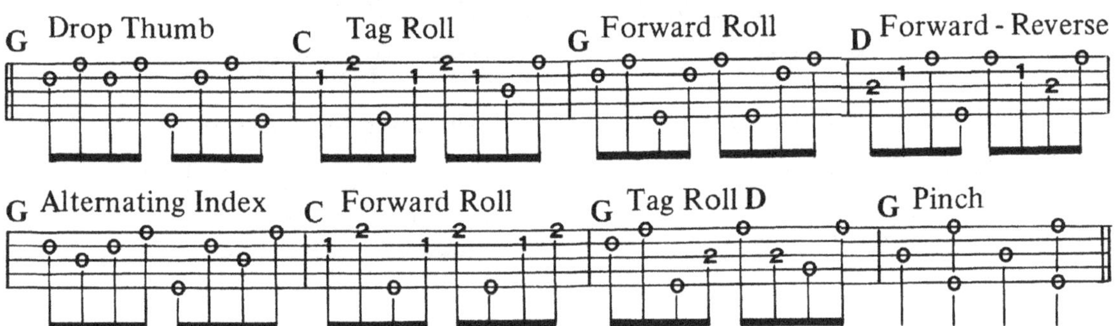

Bile Em Cabbage Down
Adding Left–Hand Techniques

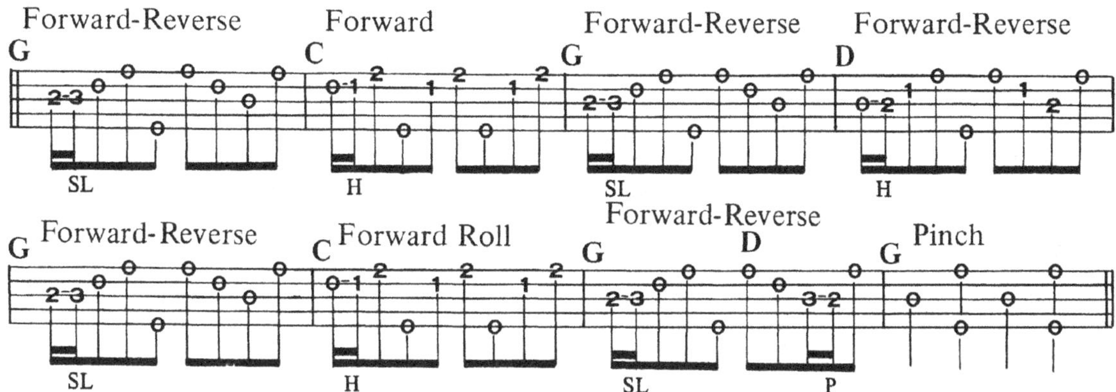

Bile Em Cabbage Down
Adding Left–Hand Techniques
And
Varying The Rhythm

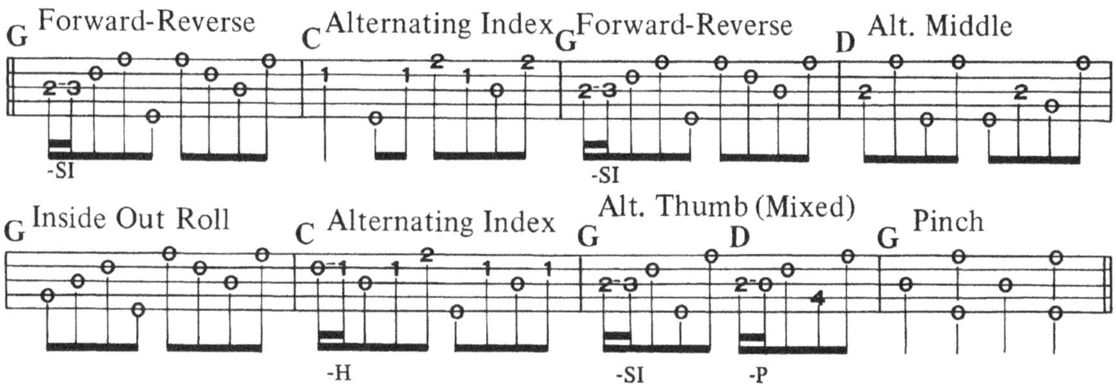

Songs
USING ROLL PATTERNS

THE GRAY GOOSE
Using The Forward Roll Pattern

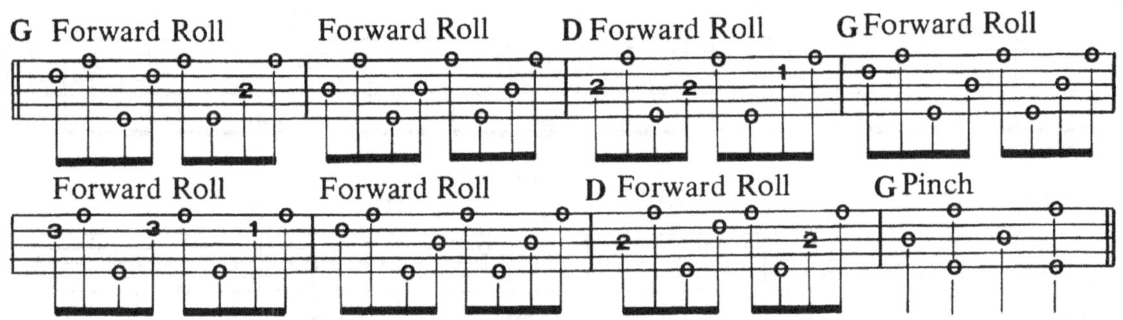

GOODNIGHT LADIES
Using Basic Roll Patterns

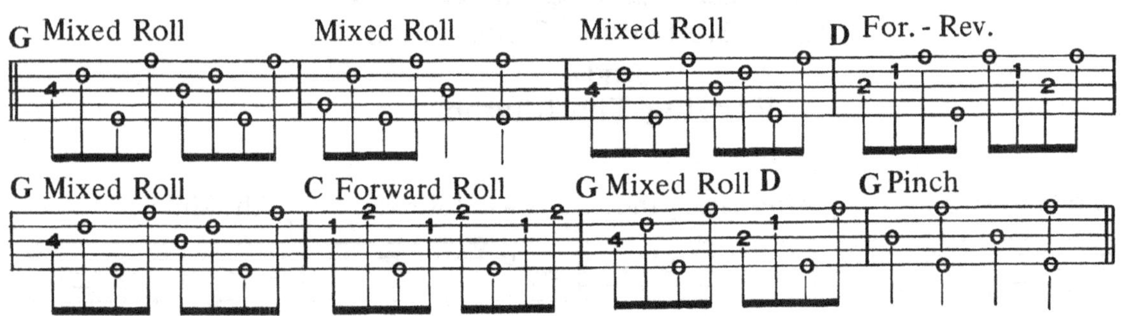

OLD MACDONALD HAD A FARM
Using Roll Patterns

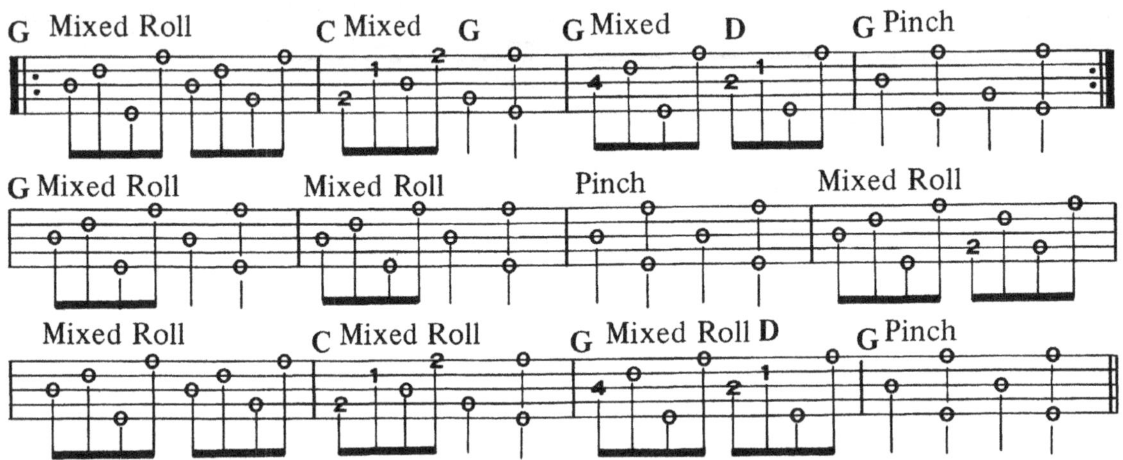

DO LORD, OH DO LORD
USING ROLL PATTERNS

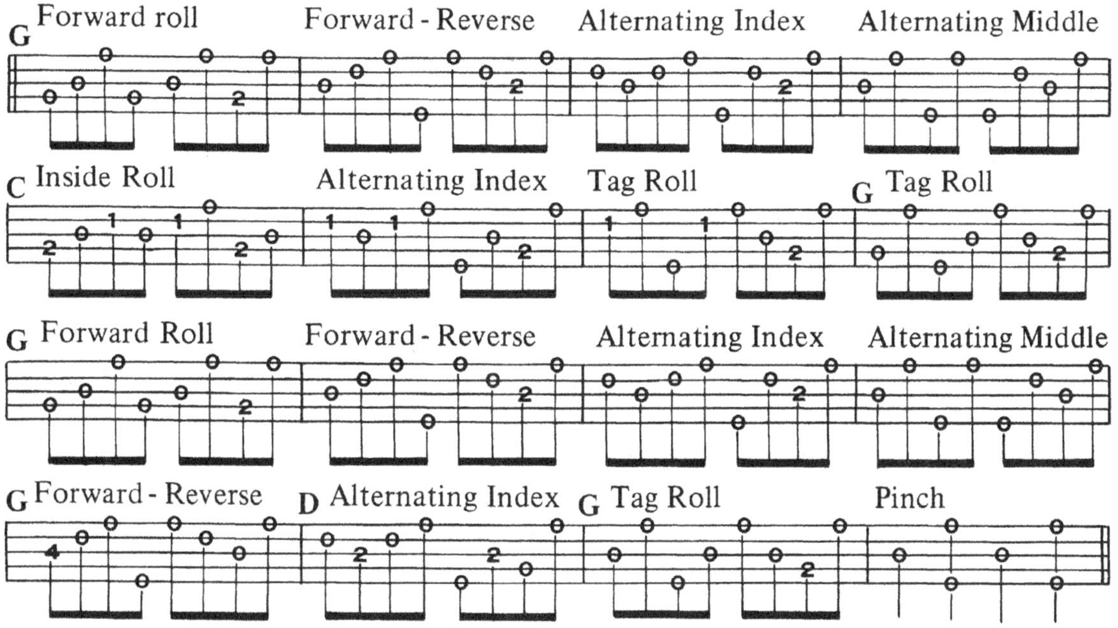

MAY I SLEEP IN YOUR BARN TONIGHT, MISTER?
USING ROLL PATTERNS

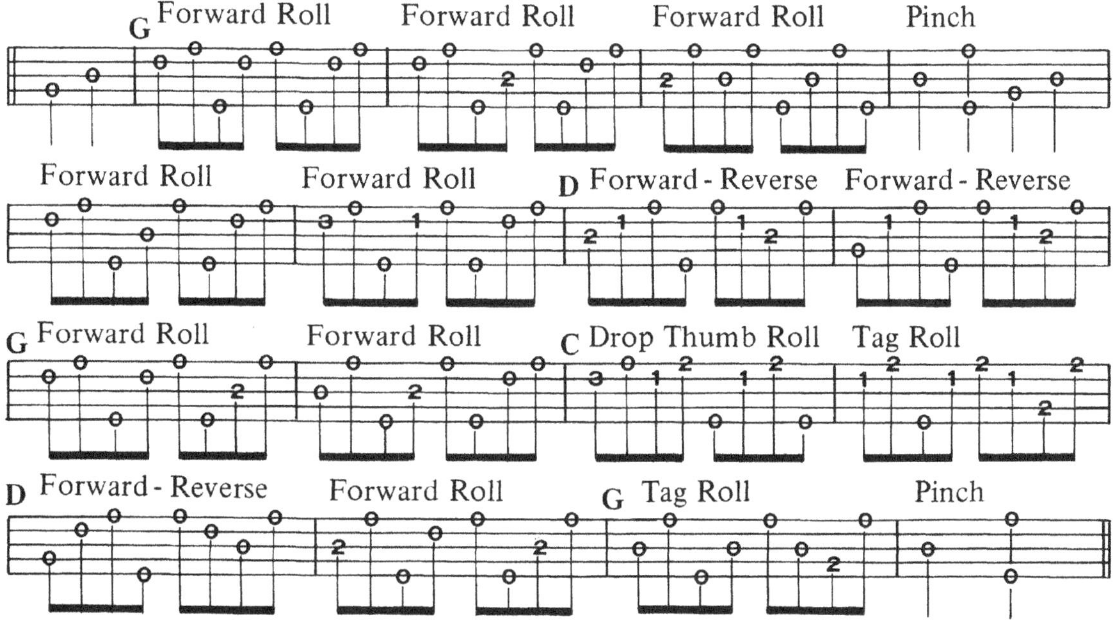

BULLY OF THE TOWN
ROLL PATTERNS WITH LEFT-HAND TECHNIQUES
AND RHYTHMIC VARIATIONS

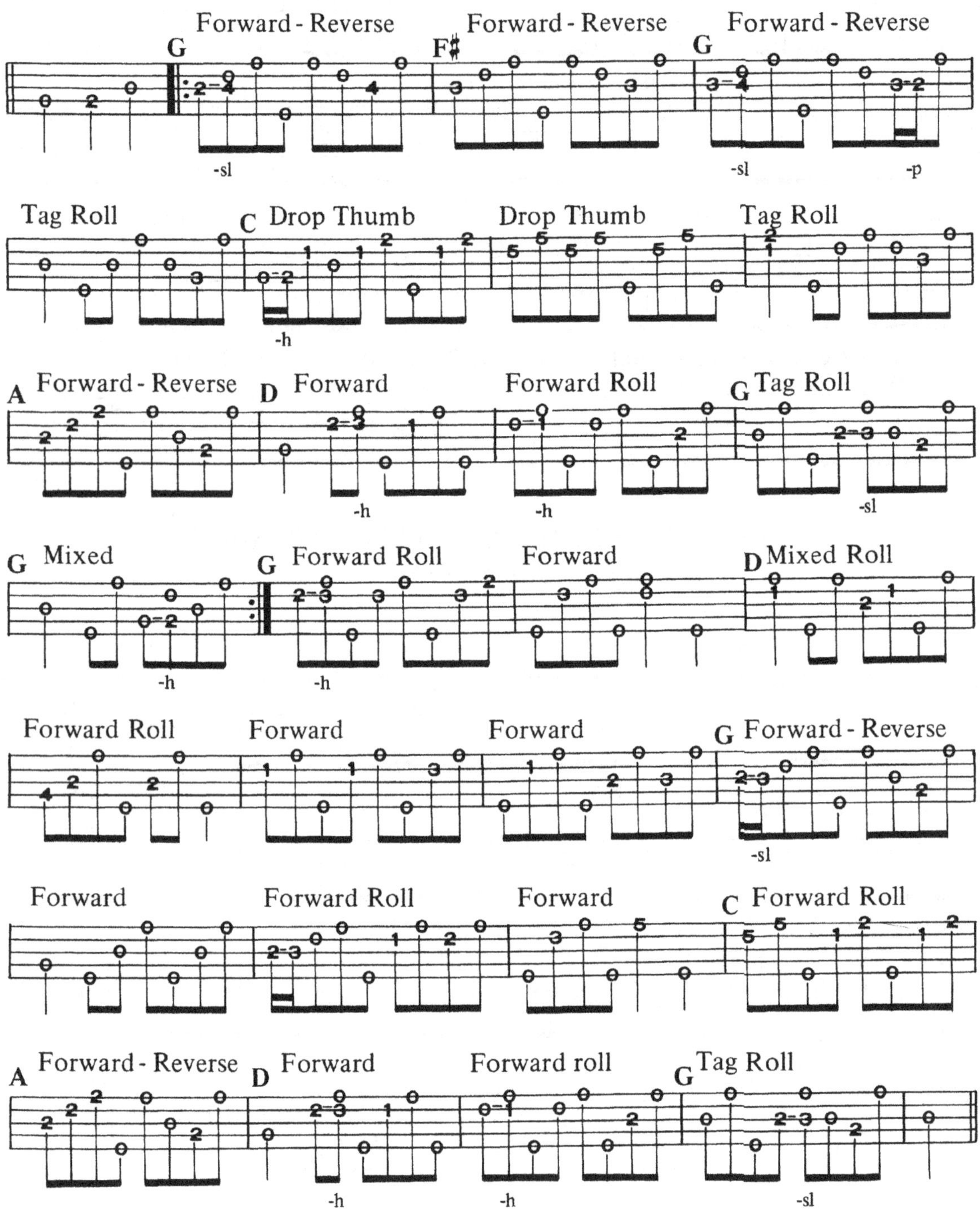

Intros

INTROS: A brief group of notes used to begin an arrangement.

These are usually referred to as "pickup notes".

TO THE G CHORD:

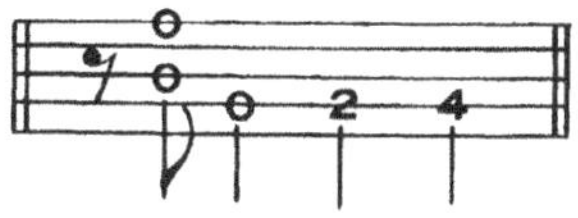
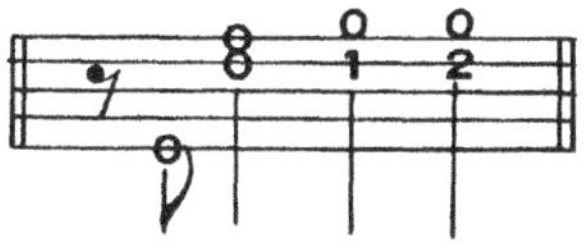
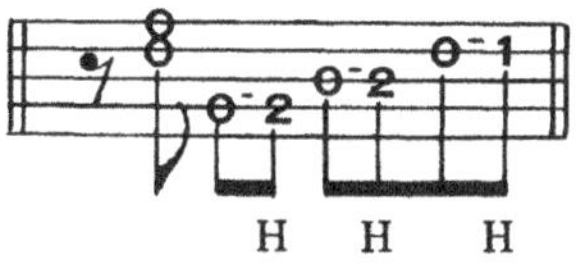

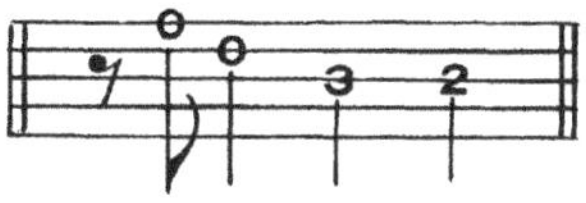
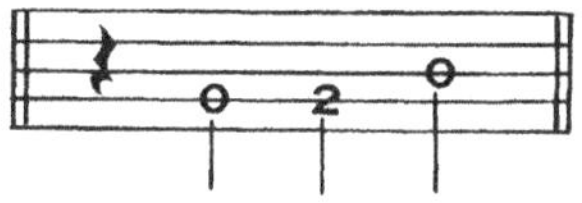
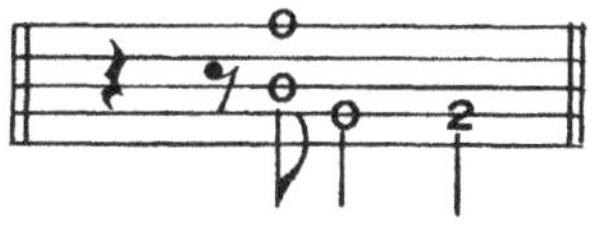
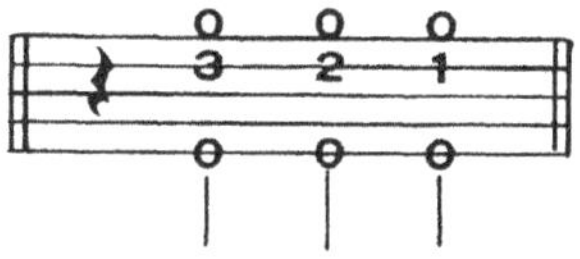
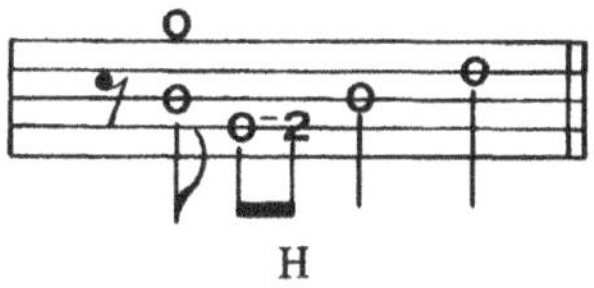

TO THE C CHORD:

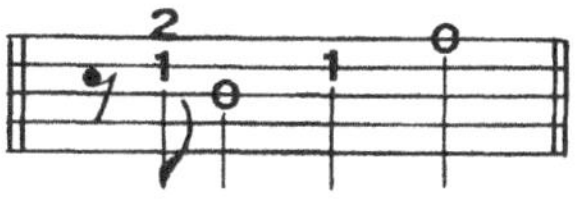
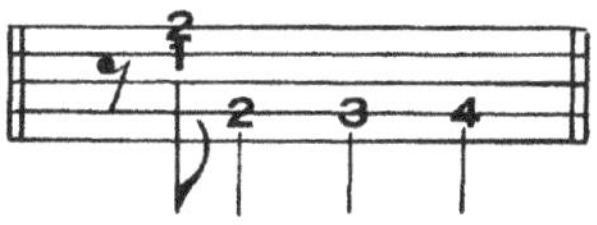
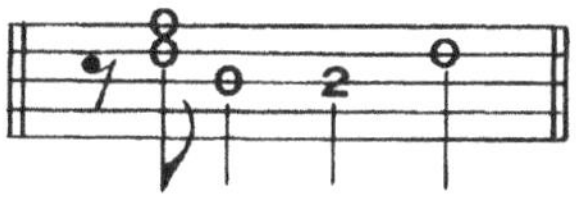

to C or G:

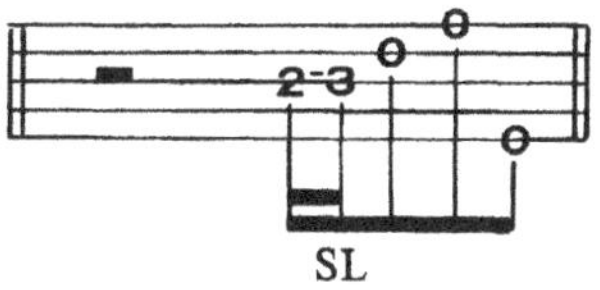

TO THE D CHORD:

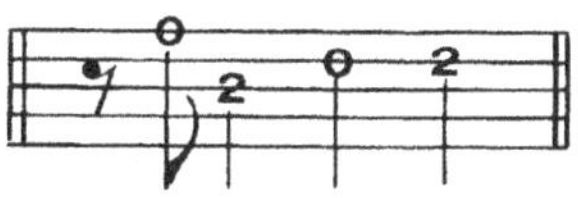
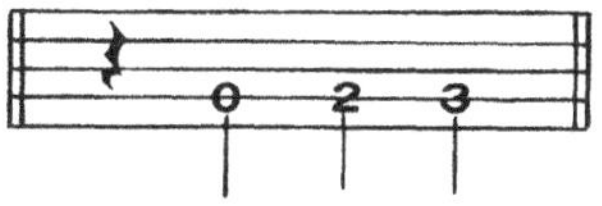

NOTES:
1.) Intros are chosen according to the chord the intro is leading into.
2.) Often the intro belongs to the V chord of the key of the song.

Licks

LICK: A lick is a fancy roll pattern, which includes lefthand tech-niques, (slides, hammers, pull-offs, chokes, etc.).

Each lick is played only for a specific chord.

G CHORD LICKS:

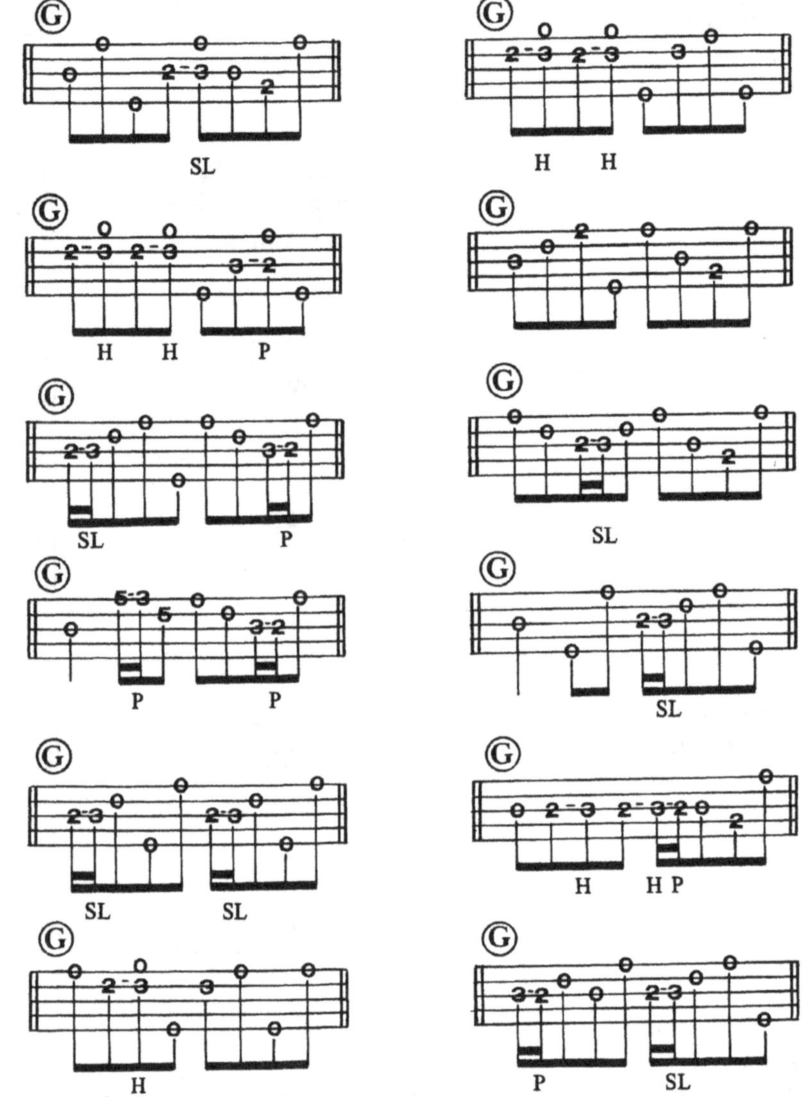

NOTES:

1.) You can improvise for any song, simply by combining any assortment of licks, according to the chords for the song. (To bring out the melody, the first note of the lick should be a melody note.)
2.) Remember -- licks are still roll patterns, but they are used only for a specific chord; roll patterns can be played with any chord.

C CHORD LICKS:

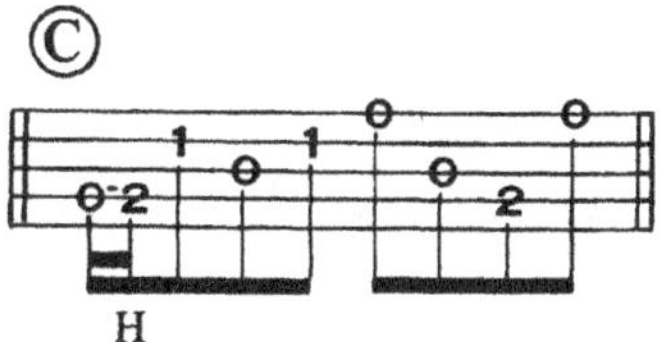
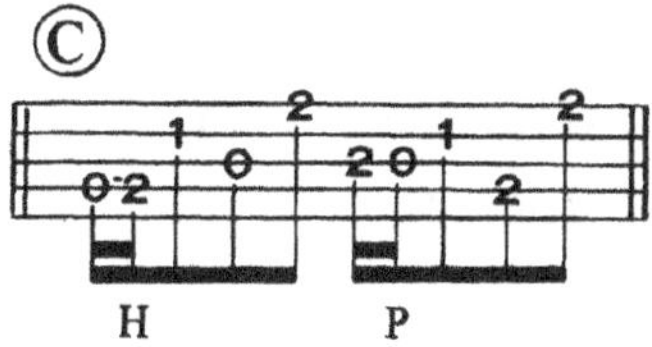

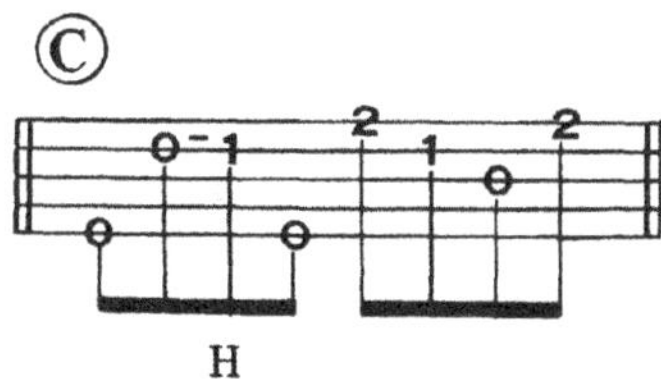
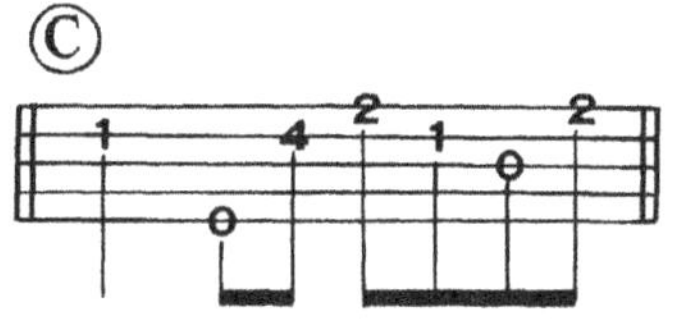

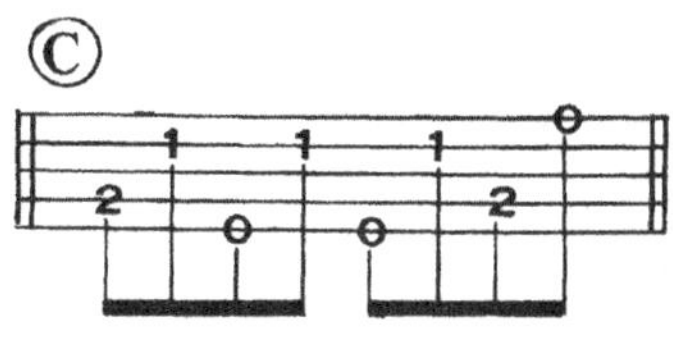
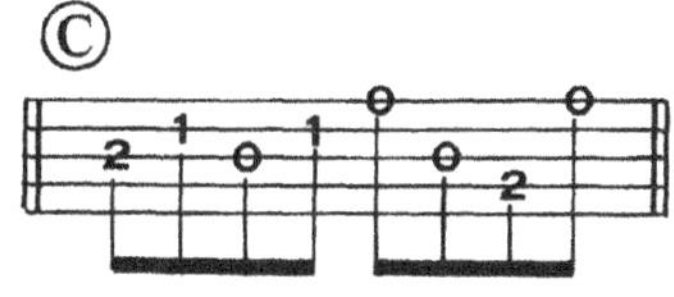

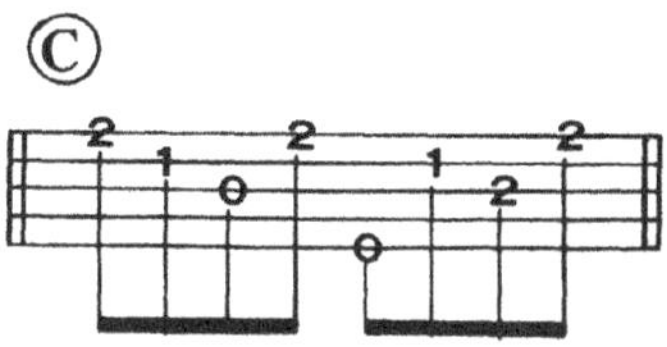
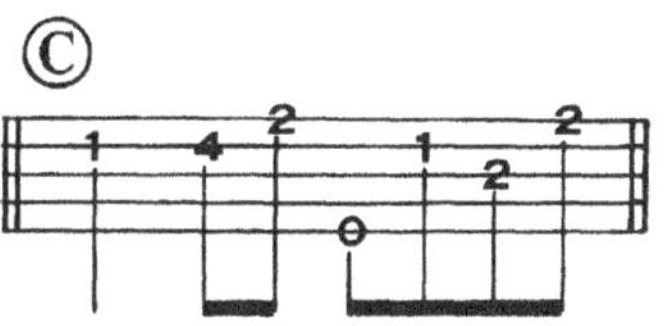

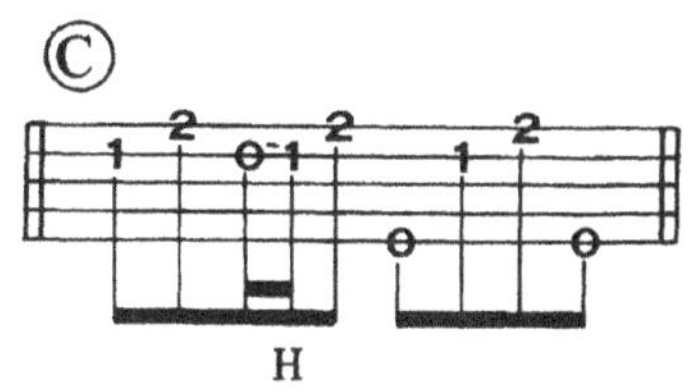
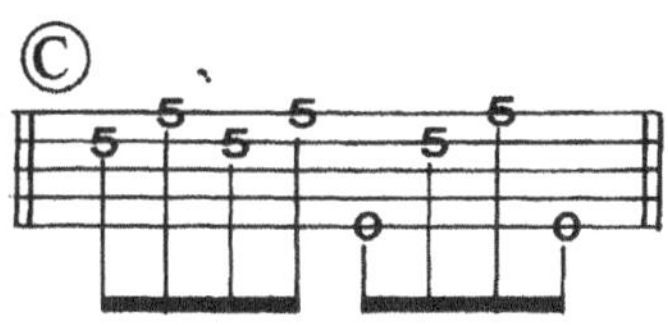

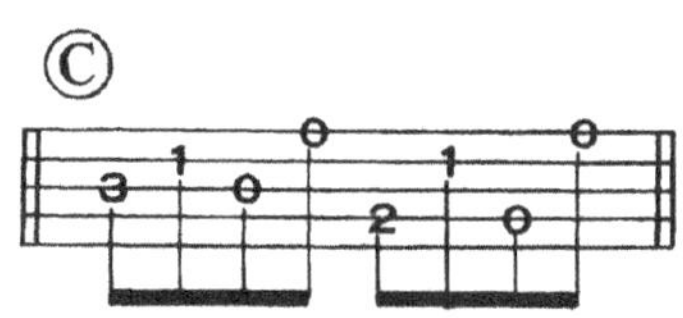

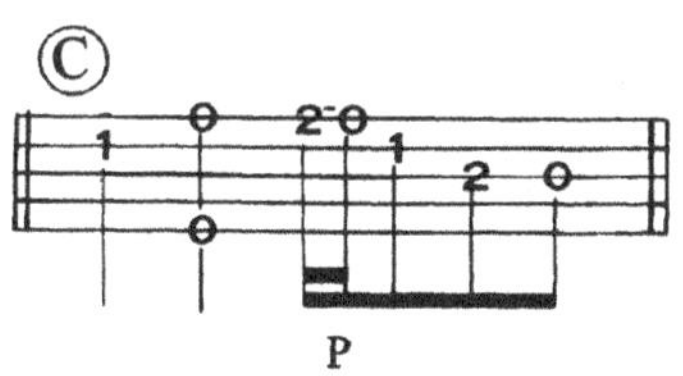
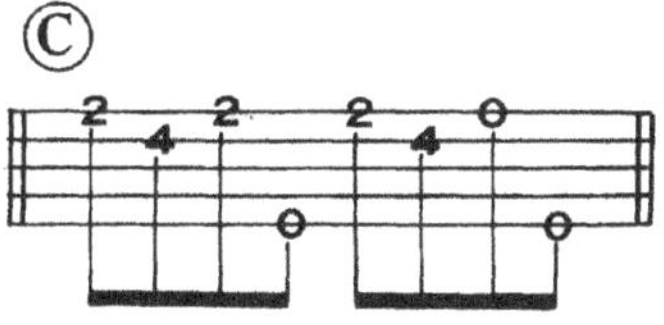

**TWO-MEASURE
C LICKS:**

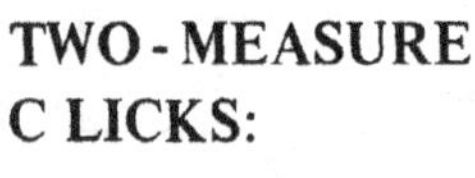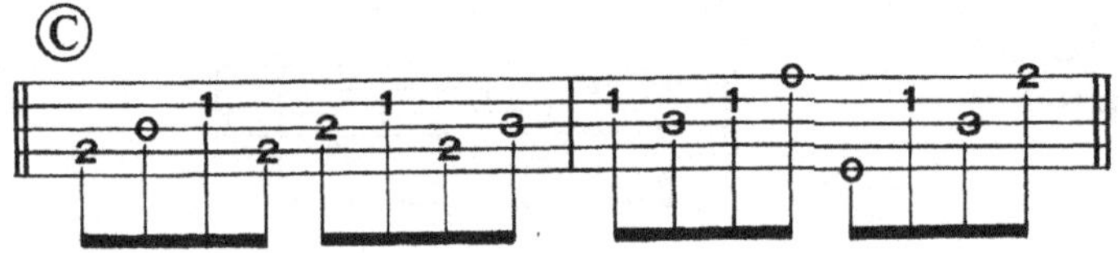

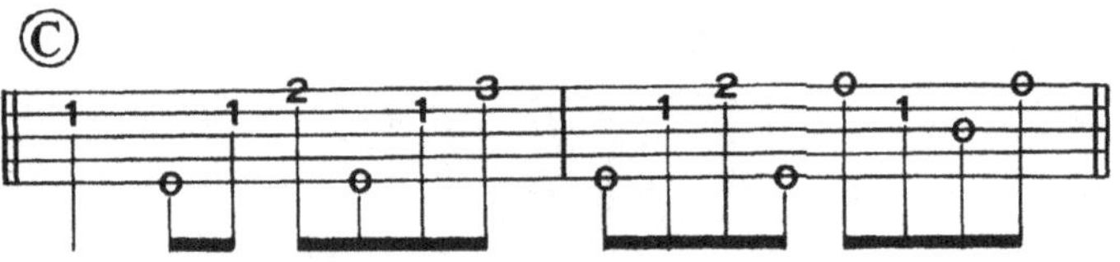

**D CHORD
LICKS:**

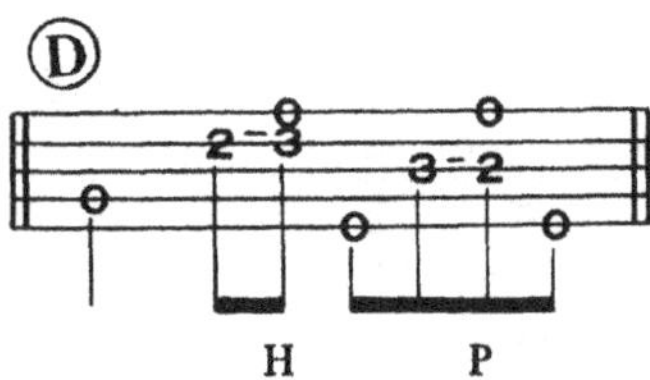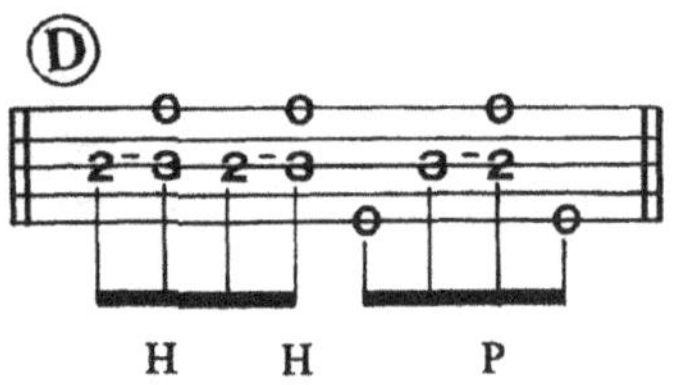

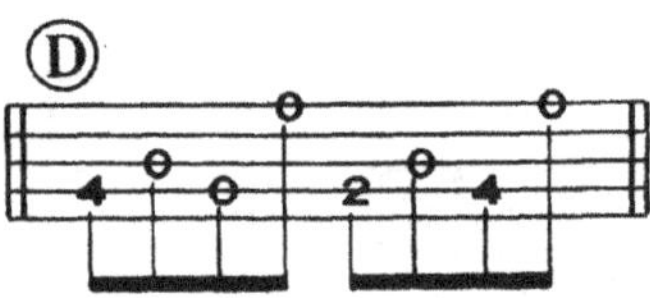

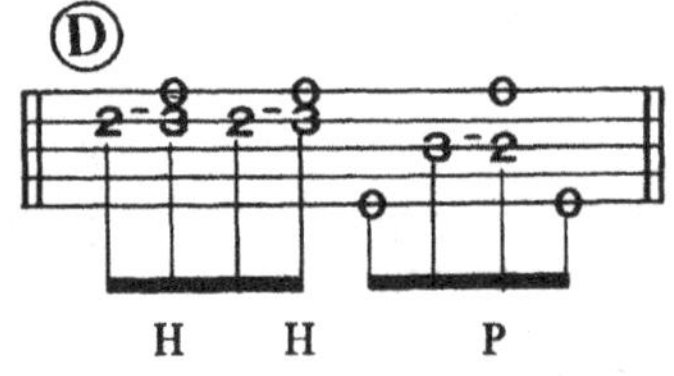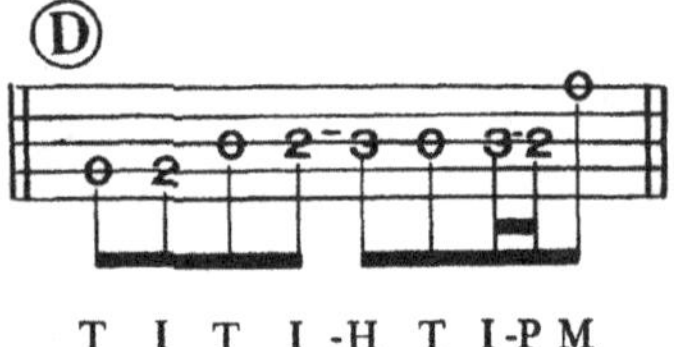

**TWO-MEASURE
D LICKS:**

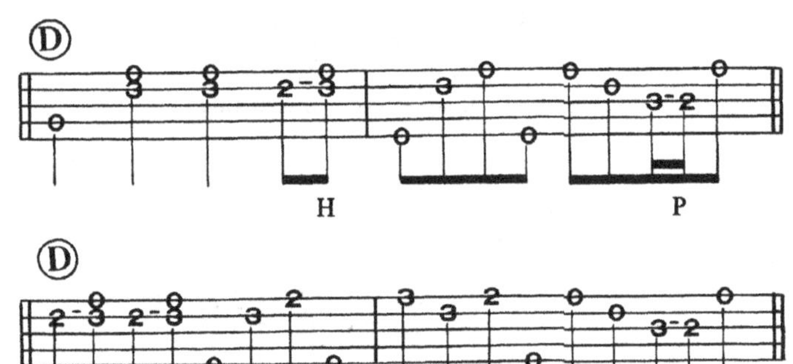

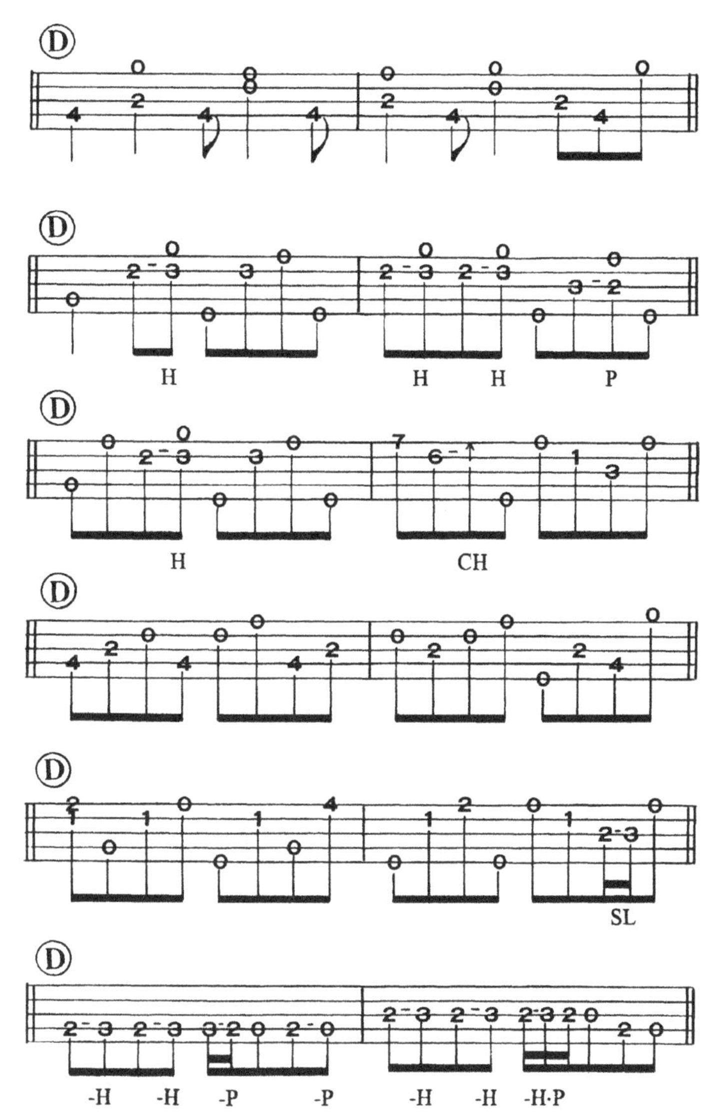

A CHORD
LICKS:

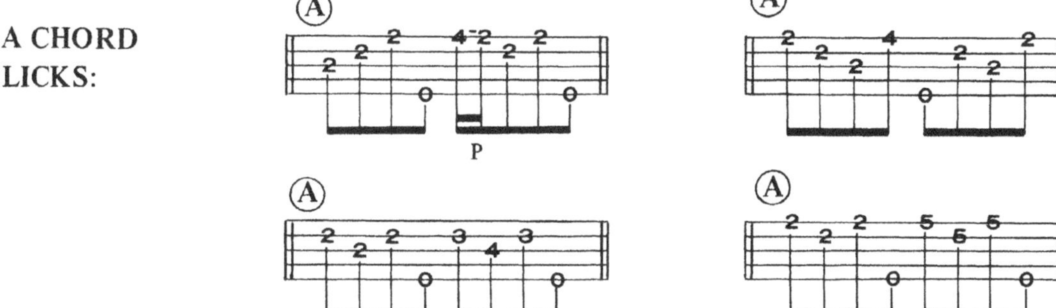

A
A
A
A
F CHORD LICKS:
F
F
F
F
P
H
B CHORD LICKS:
B
B
B
B
E CHORD LICKS:
E
E
E
E

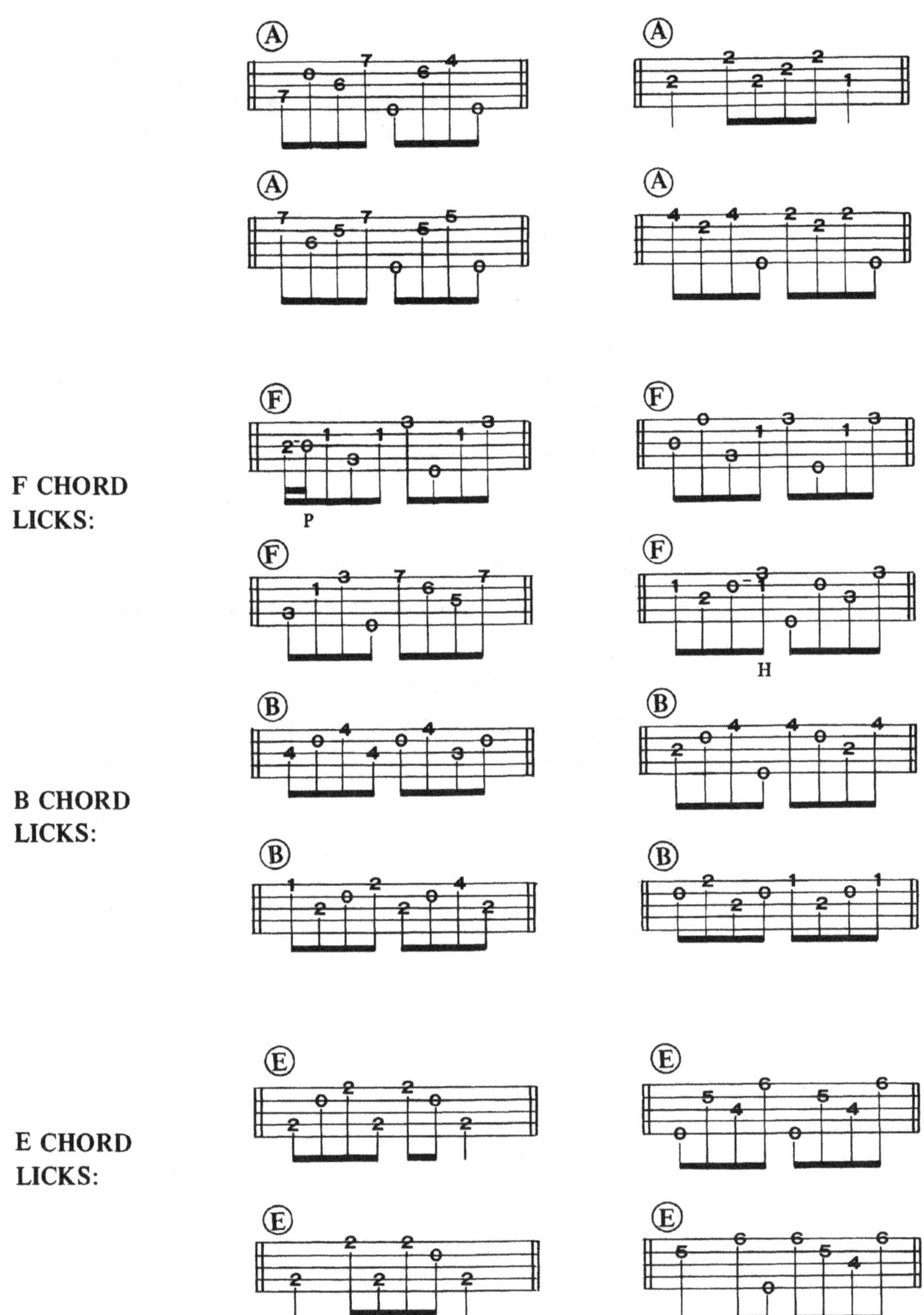

40

Songs
USING LICKS

LITTLE MAGGIE

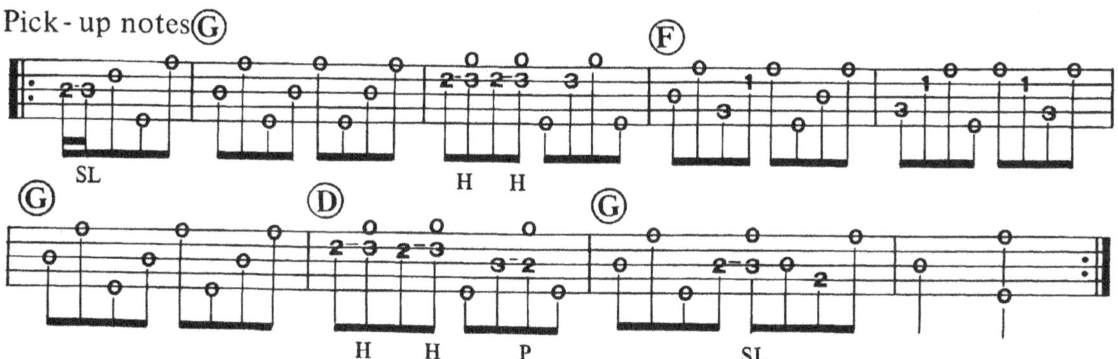

VARIATION:

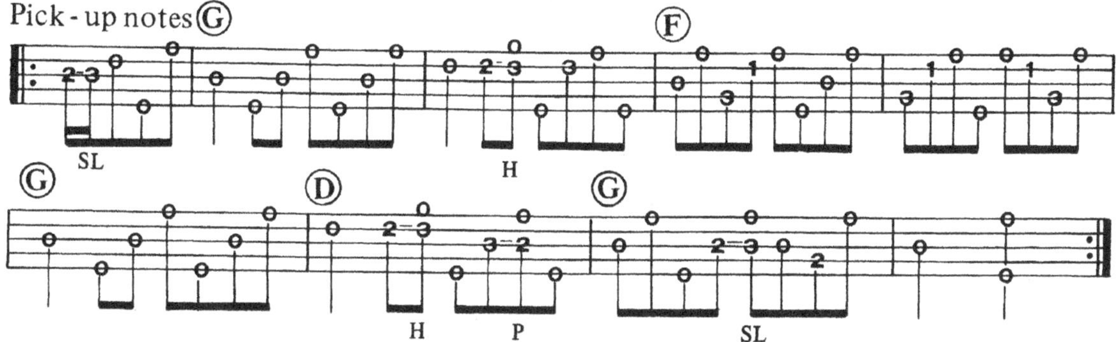

VARIATION:

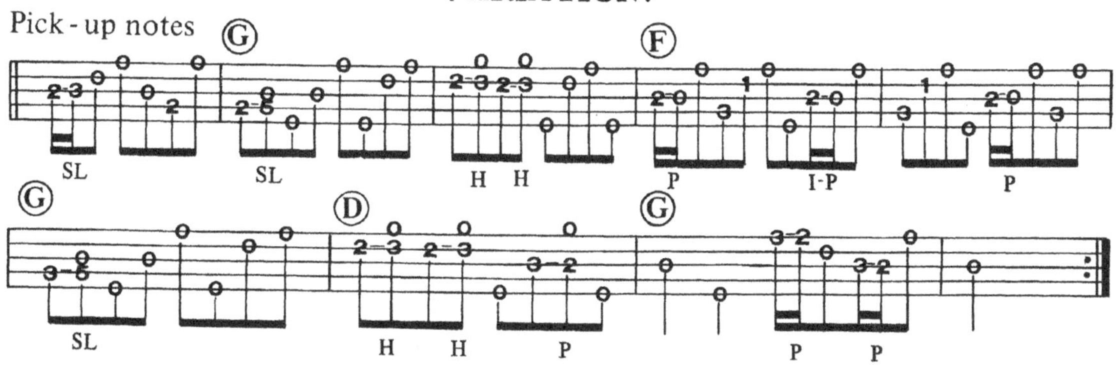

NOTES:

1. You can use any combination of rolls, or rolls and licks, or only licks to improvise an arrangement for any song, as long as you apply them to the right chords.
2. Fiddler's often play this tune in the Key of A; place your capo on the 2nd fret to raise the pitch of your banjo to the Key of A.

CRIPPLE CREEK

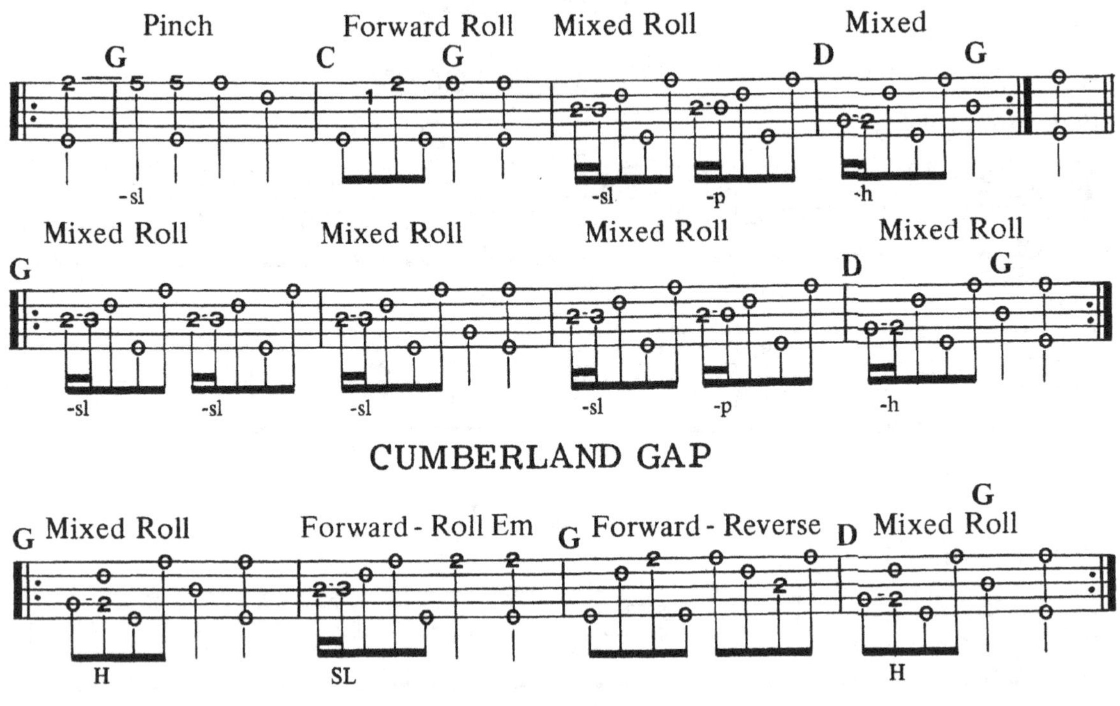

CUMBERLAND GAP

WILDWOOD FLOWER

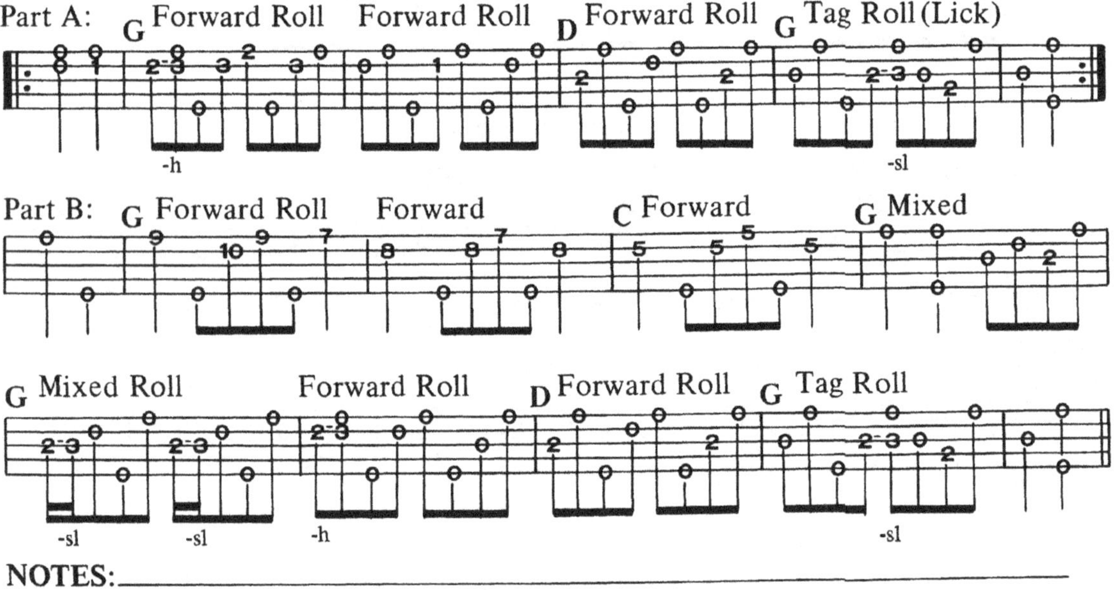

NOTES:

1.) Remember -- licks are really roll patterns which include left - hand techniques and/or rhythmic variations.

MAMA DON'T ALLOW

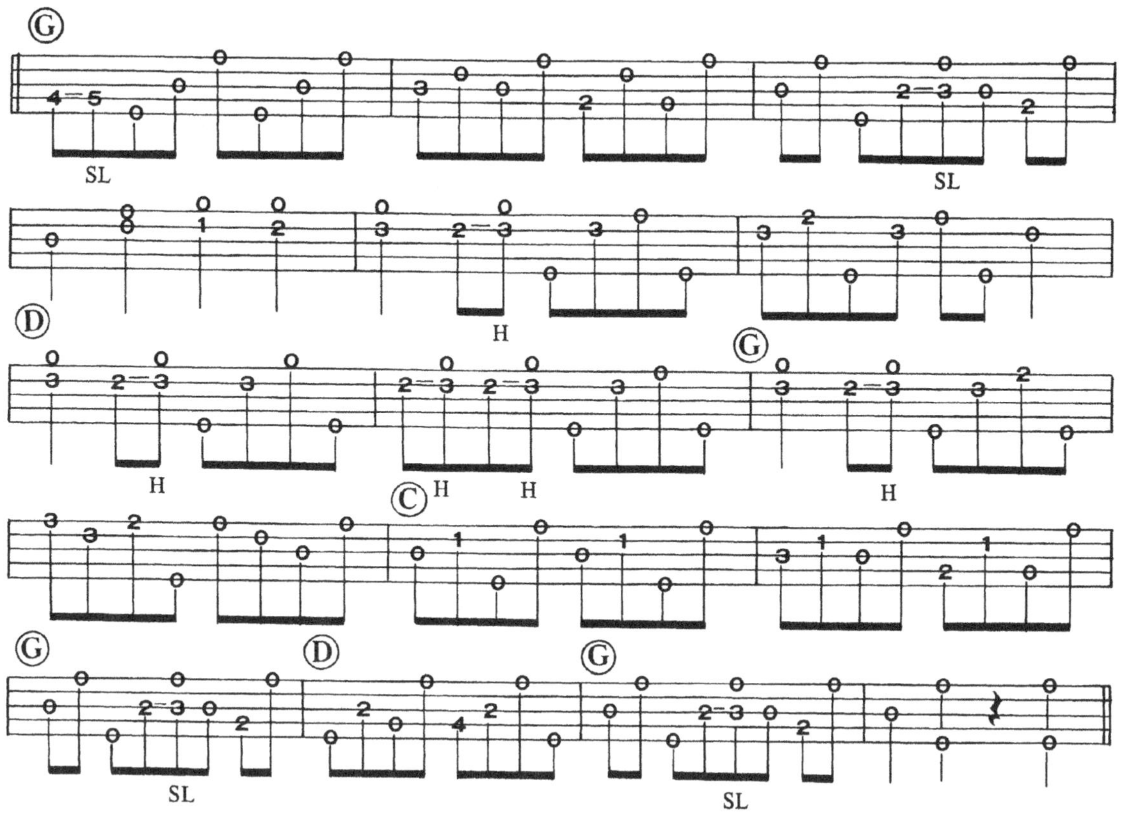

WRECK OF THE OLD '97

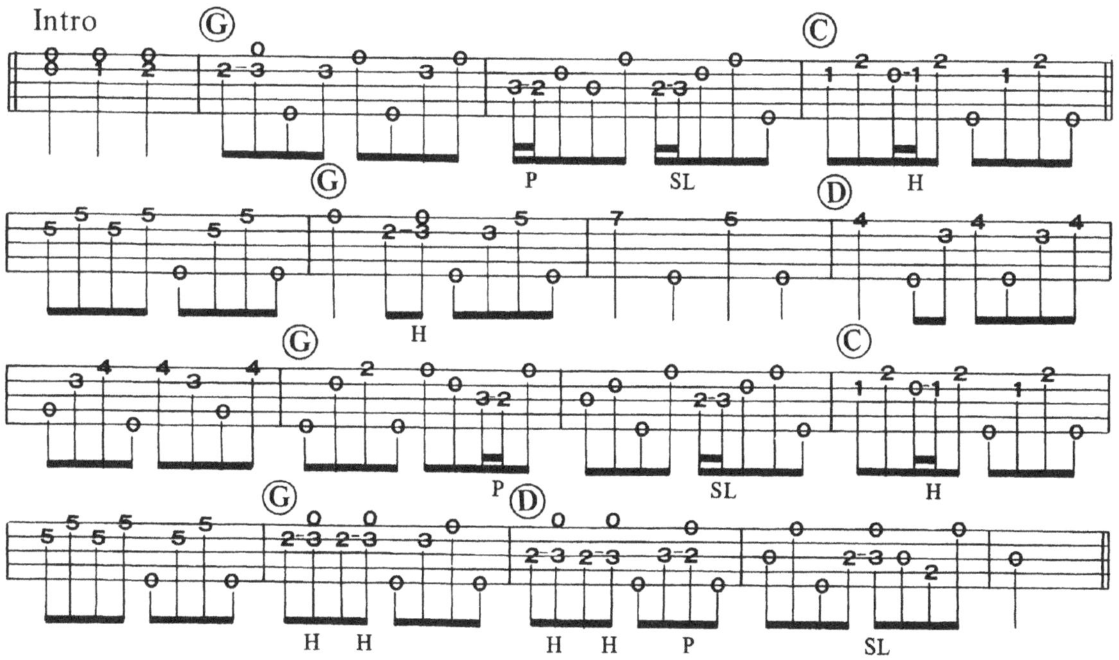

Up-The-Neck

Up-the-neck usually refers to the 5th-22nd fret area of the fingerboard of the banjo.

The right hand is usually positioned close to the fingerboard, away from the bridge.

IN THIS SECTION:

    Introduction

    Intros (Pick up Notes)

    Up - The Neck Licks

    Songs

Up-The-Neck
INTRODUCTION

Up-the-neck usually refers to the 5th-22nd fret area of the fingerboard.

CHORDS ARE IMPORTANT: The left hand usually works from chord positions when songs are played up the neck of the banjo.

USING ROLL PATTERNS: By playing roll patterns with the right hand, while holding the appropriate chords with the left hand, you can improvise an up-the-neck arrangement for any song.

USING LICKS: You can also play any song up-the-neck of the banjo by playing an assortment of up-the-neck licks, (your choice). Remember, licks must be played for the correct chords.

ROLLS & LICKS: Usually songs are played with a combination of rolls and licks while the left hand holds chord positions, moving the fingers out of these positions only to reach the non-chord tones required or desired.

NOTES:

1.) The right hand usually picks the strings in the "Y" POSITION of the head of the banjo, close to the fingerboard, away from the bridge, in order to produce a more mellow tone, when playing up-the-neck with the left hand.
2.) See pp. 19-25 for complete Chord Charts.
3.) See pp. 28-29 for examples of Roll Patterns.

Intros

UP-THE-NECK

INTROS: These are usually referred to as "pick up notes".

Intros played up-the-neck usually lead into a certain chord position.

Intros are used to begin arrangements.

TO THE G CHORD:

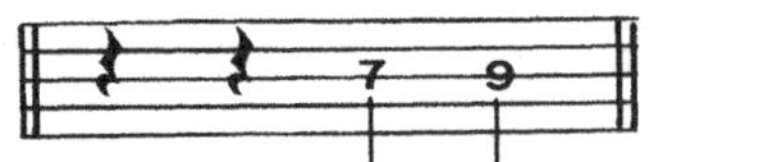
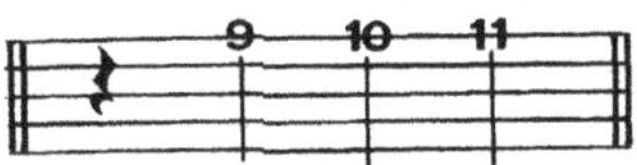

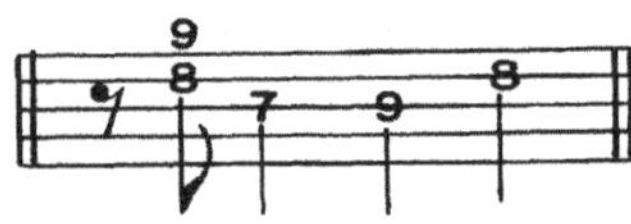

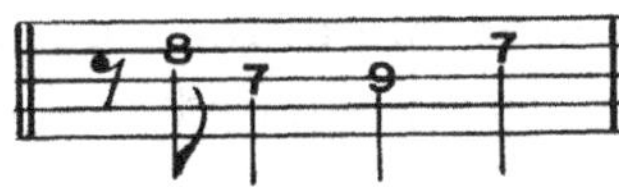
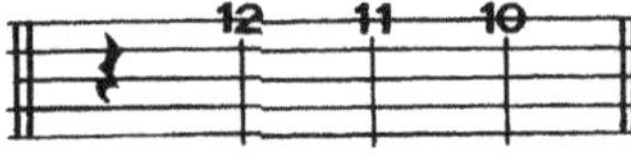

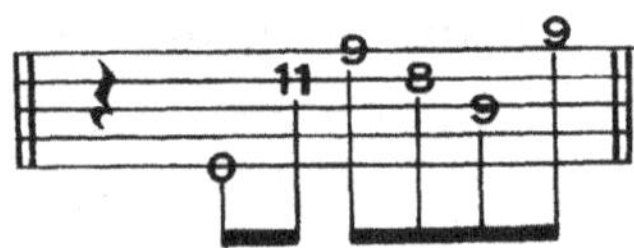
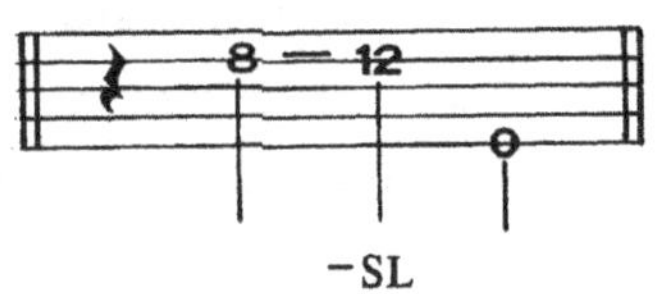

TO THE C CHORD:

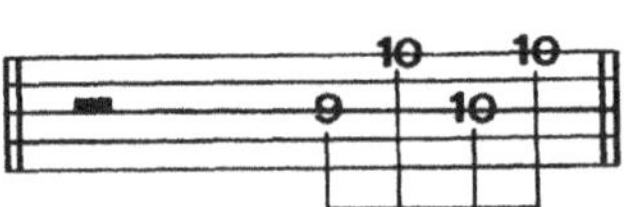
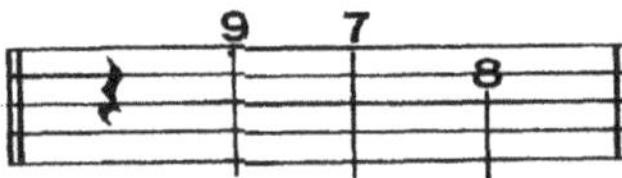

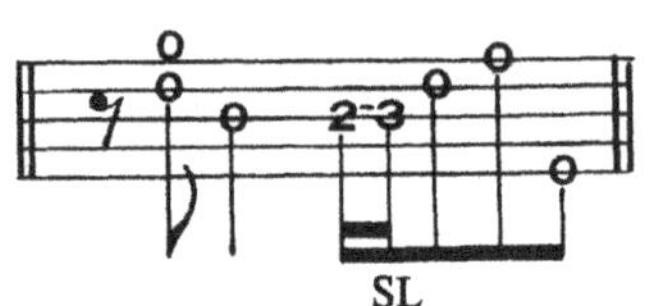

Up-The-Neck Licks

You can vary the songs you already play, or improvise with a new arrange-ment, by substituting different licks in your arrangements for songs.

G CHORD LICKS:

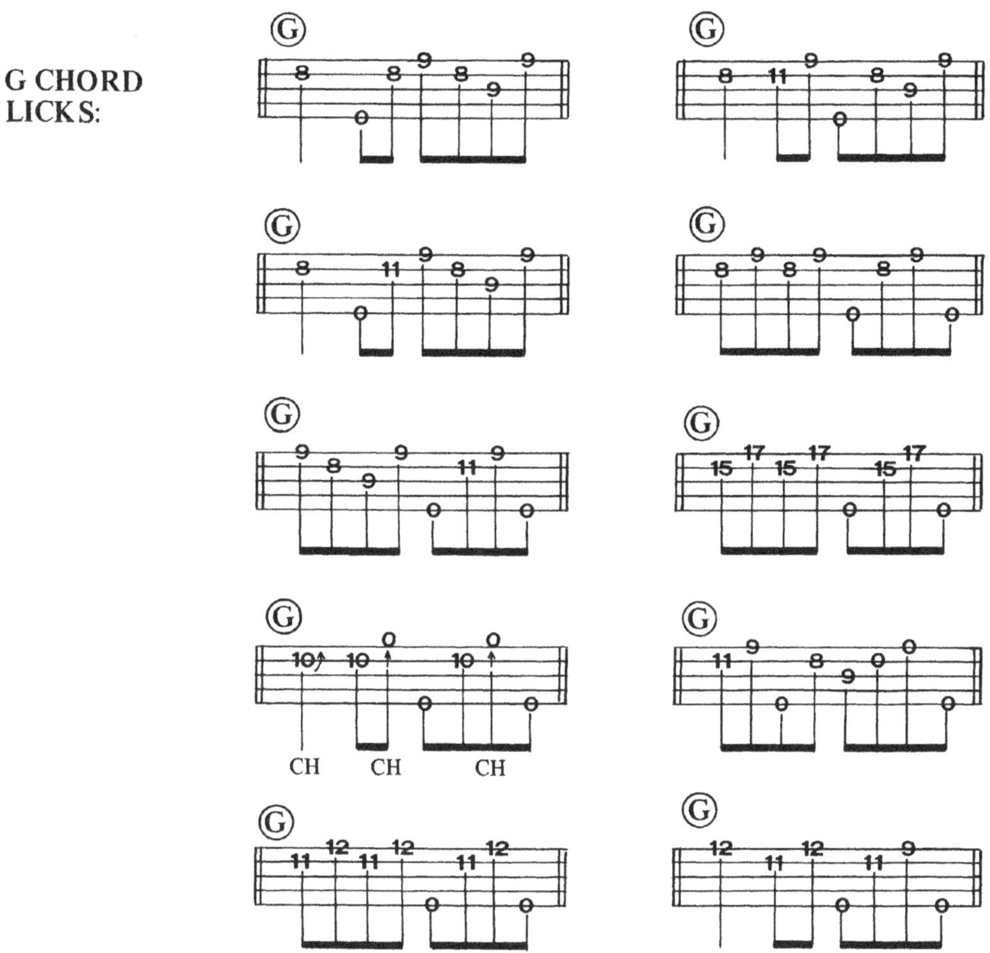

1.) Most of the up-the-neck licks require holding a chord position with the left hand.
2.) Many up-the-neck licks are patterns which can be played for any chord.

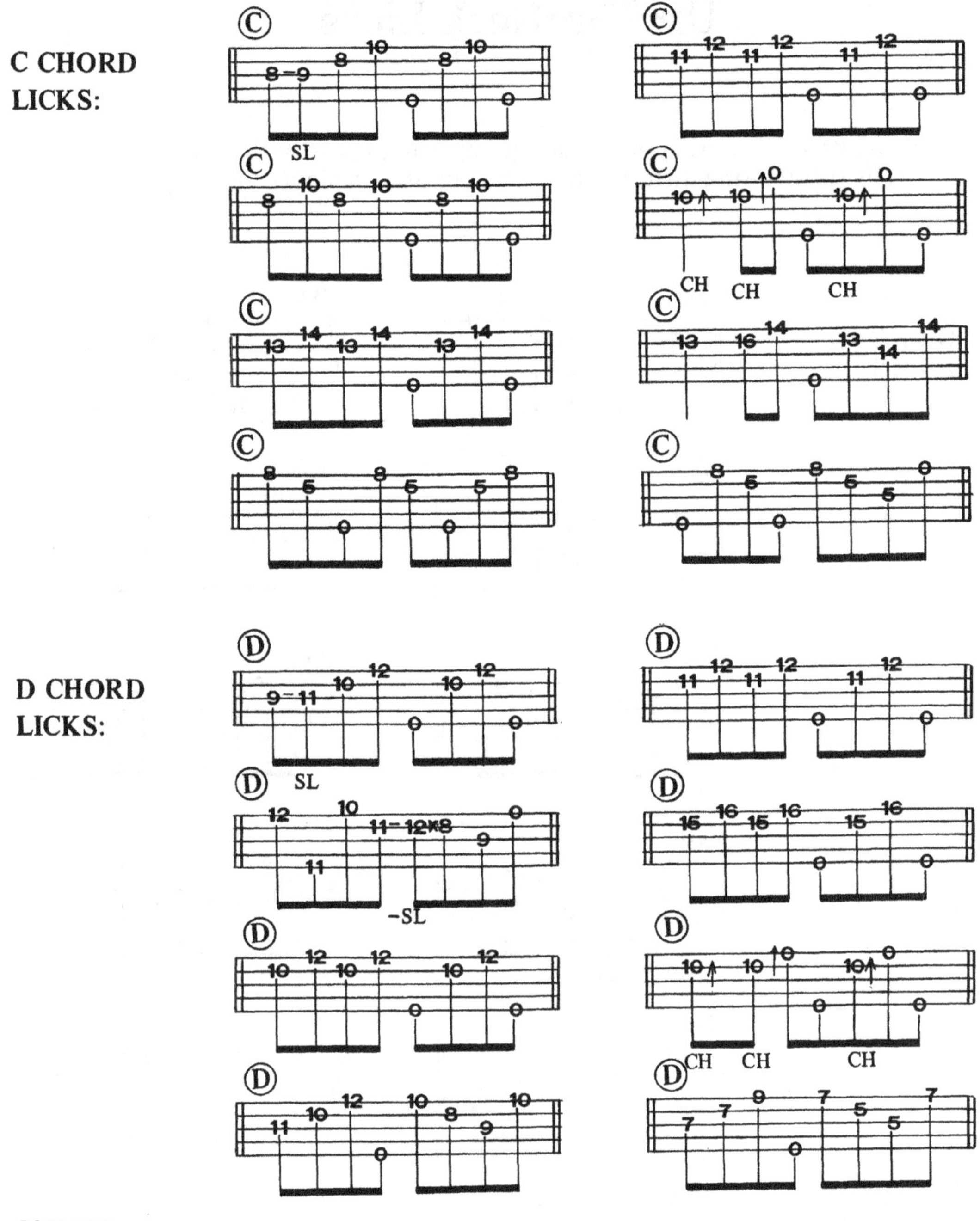

NOTES: ____

1.) Notice that some licks work for more than one chord. The tones used in these licks belong to each chord in some manner, (as 7ths, b3rds, etc.)

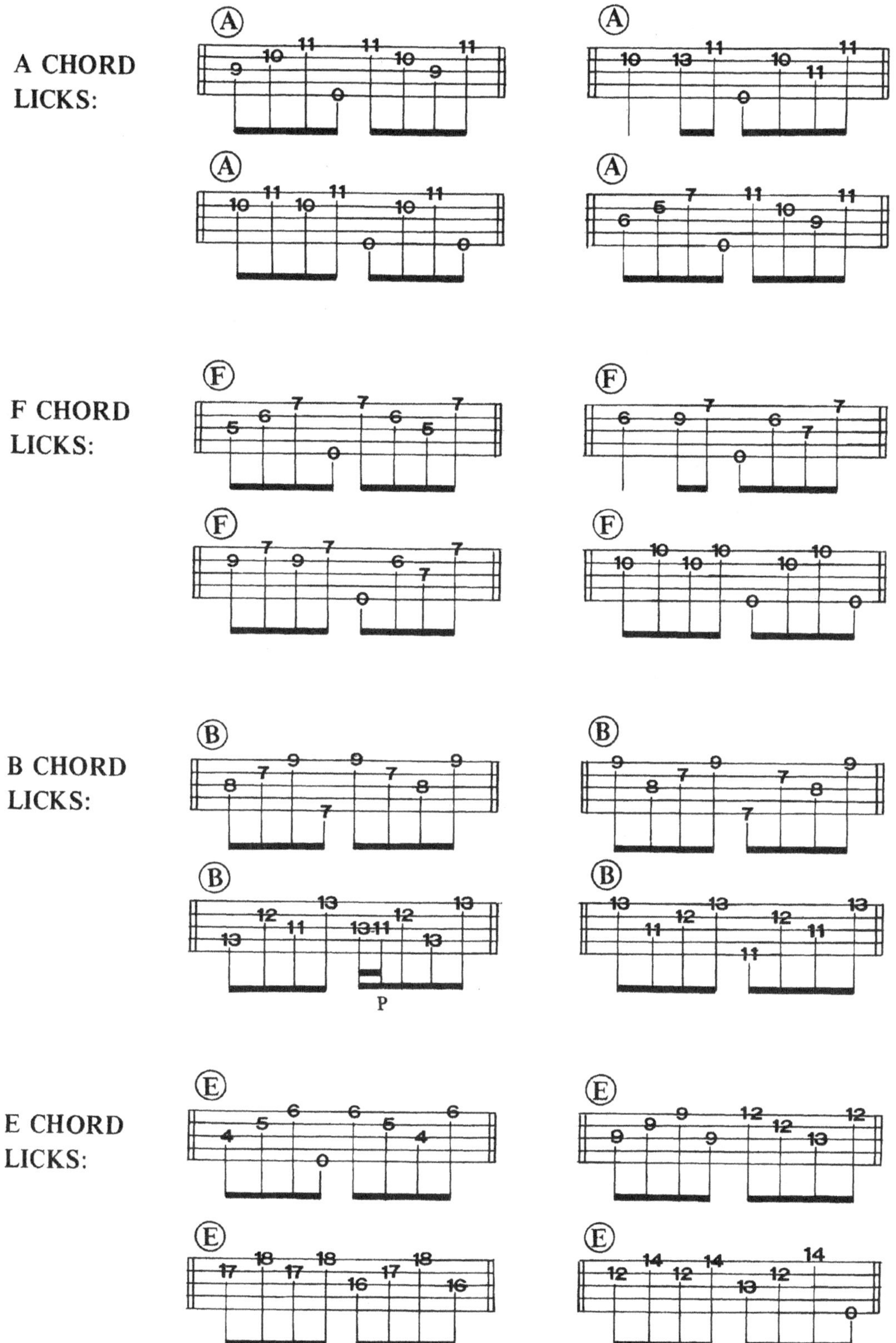

A CHORD LICKS:
F CHORD LICKS:
B CHORD LICKS:
E CHORD LICKS:

Songs

USING UP-THE-NECK LICKS

BILE EM CABBAGE DOWN

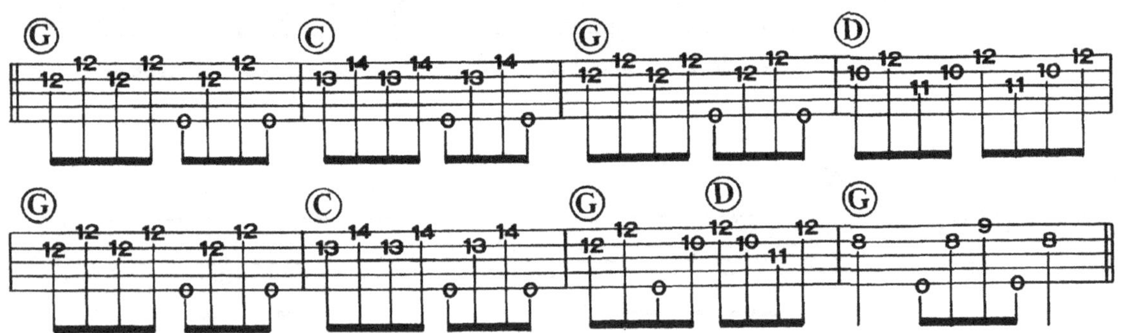

VARIATION

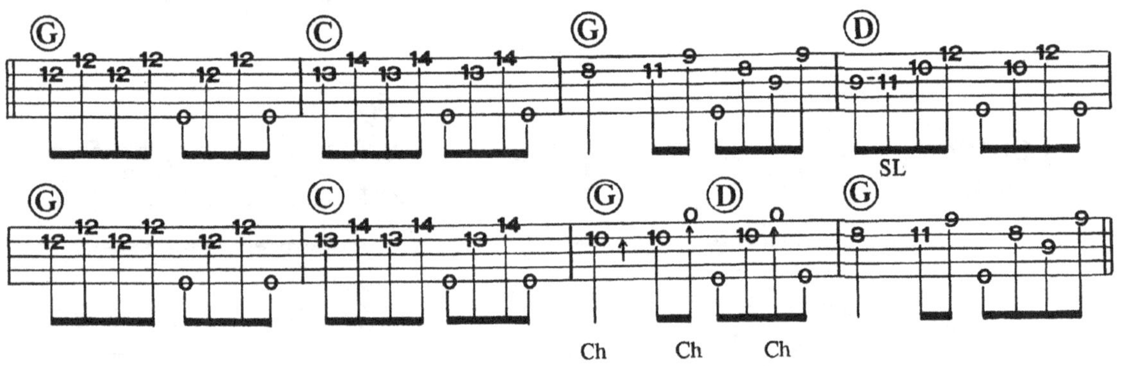

CUMBERLAND GAP

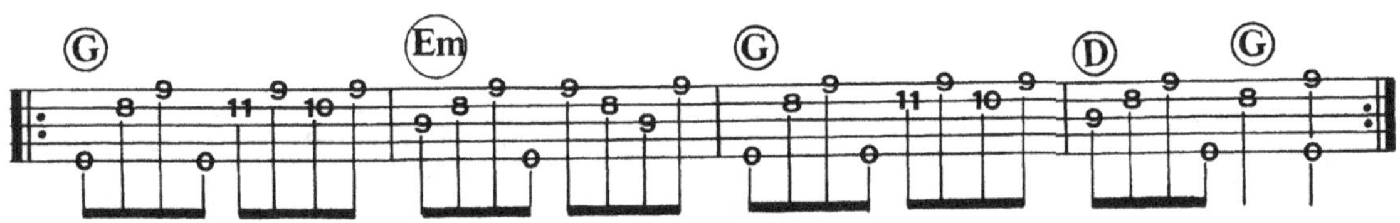

NOTES:

1.) For down-the-neck arrangements, (played with the lower-pitched tones) for these songs, see pp. 30-43.

LITTLE MAGGIE

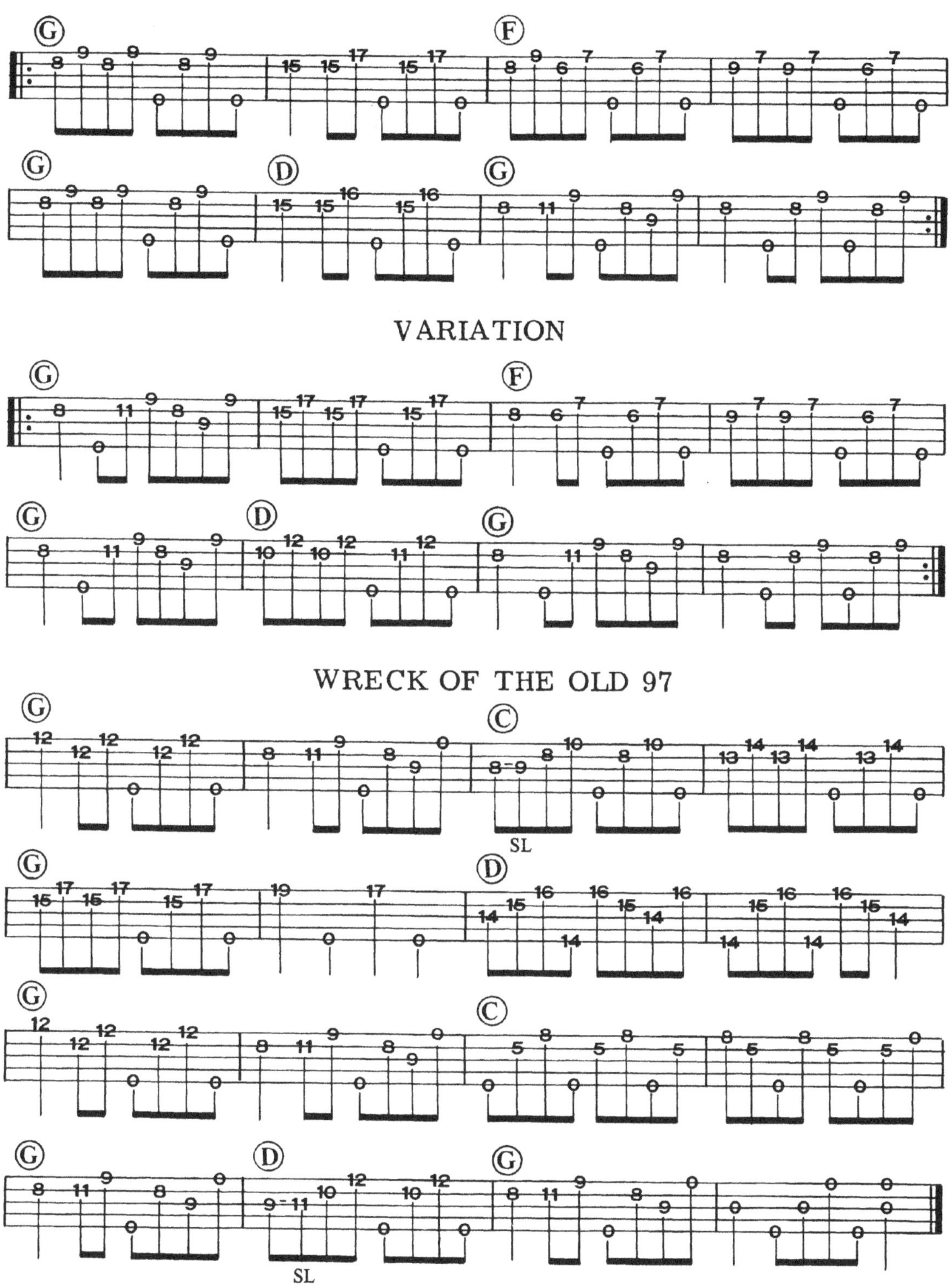

VARIATION

WRECK OF THE OLD 97

MAMA DON'T ALLOW

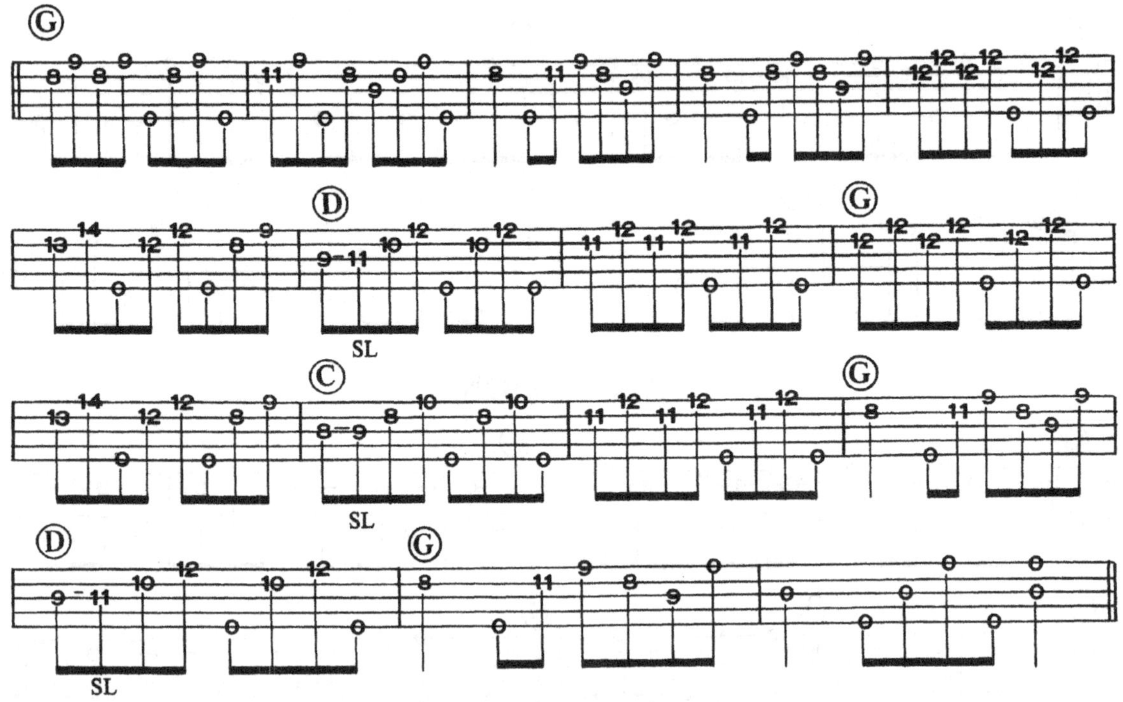

SHE'LL BE COMING AROUND THE MOUNTAIN

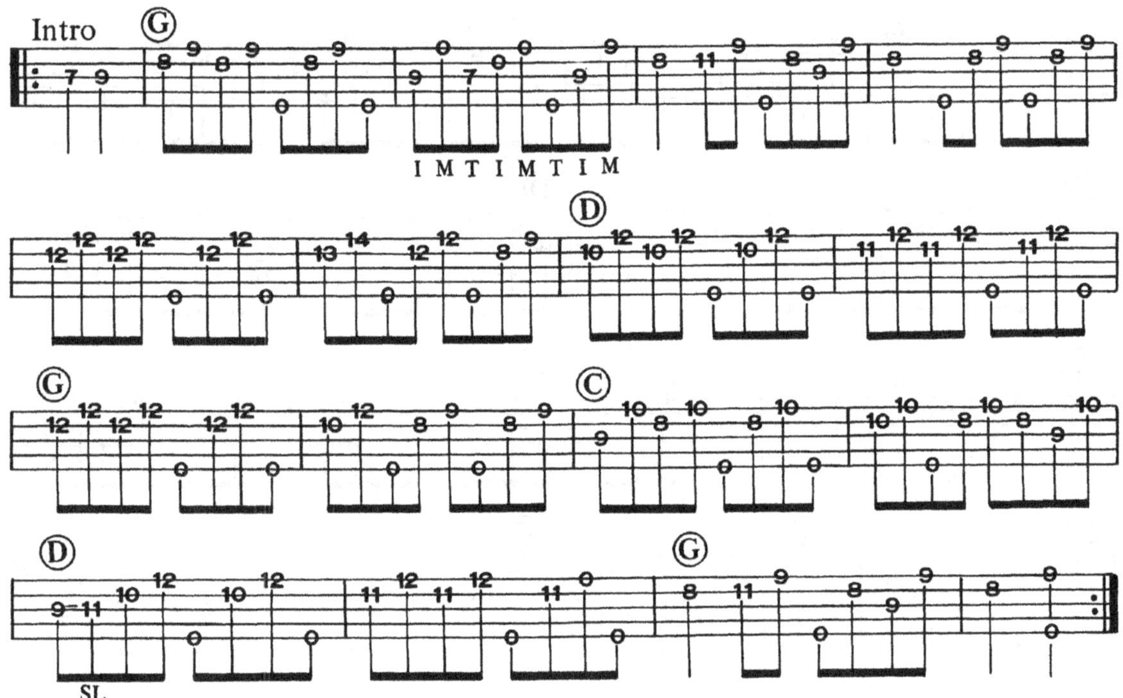

The Melodic Style

This style of playing dates back to the early 1900's when classical music was popular on the banjo. However, Bill Keith and Bobby Thompson are generally credited with developing "Melodic style" in its current form, in the early 1960's. In the "melodic style" of playing, almost every note played is a melody note. These notes work along scale lines.

IN THIS SECTION:

Introduction

Scales & Licks

Songs

NOTES:

1.) Other terms for "Melodic style" are "fiddle style", Keith style", and "chromatic style".

Introduction

DEFINITION: Melodic style involves playing the banjo in the style of a fiddle, where almost every note played is a melody note.

SCALES: Tones from the scale line are used to fill in the spaces.

Melody notes generally work along scale lines.

DIXIE

Scruggs style using Rolls and Licks:

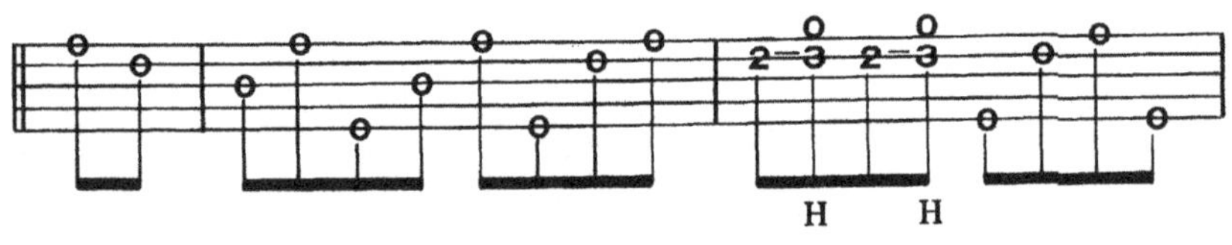

DIXIE

Melodic style using scales:

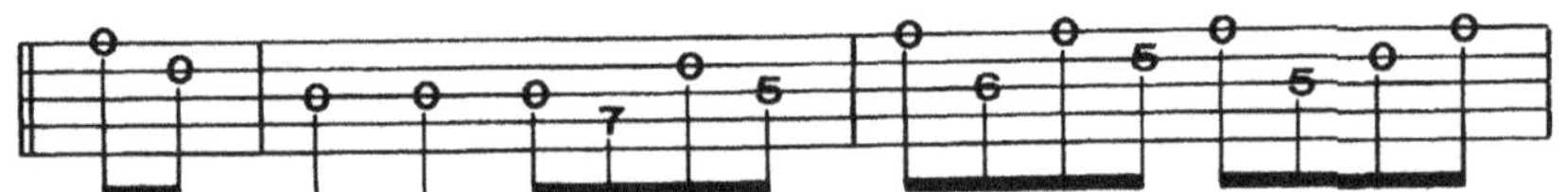

NOTES:

1.) Almost any song can be arranged for the banjo so that it can be played either in "Scruggs style" or in "Melodic style".

2.) Scruggs style uses rolls and licks. One finger plays the melody notes, while the other 2 fingers play background notes.

3.) Melodic style: almost every note played is a melody note.
Melody notes are derived from scales.

4.) You do not generally hold chord positions in the melodic style as you do when playing Scruggs style rolls. Instead, you generally hold two notes at a time from the scale line.

Scale Patterns

Melodic style playing is based upon scales. Usually, you will hold two notes at a time, rather than entire chords, with the left hand.

If a song is played in the Key of G, the melody will be picked out from the G scale. The spaces will be filled in with neighbor tones from this scale. The G Scale can be used for any chord in the Key of G, and for the G chord in any other key.

G MAJOR SCALE:

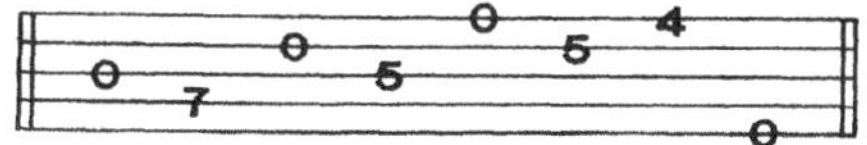

C MAJOR SCALE: The C scale can also be used for the Key of C and for the C chord in any key.

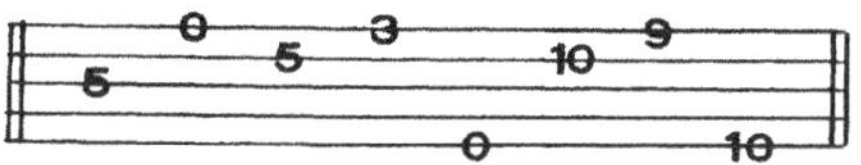

D MAJOR SCALE: The D Scale can be used for the Key of D, and for the D chord.

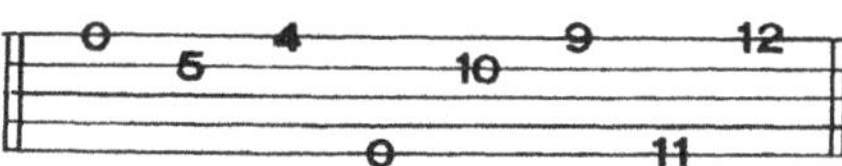

A MAJOR SCALE:

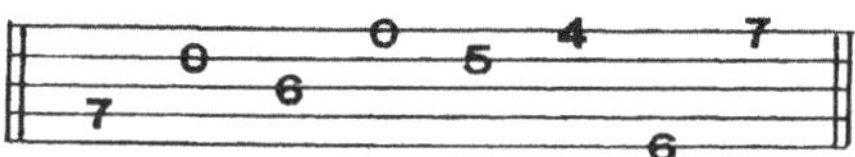

F MAJOR SCALE:

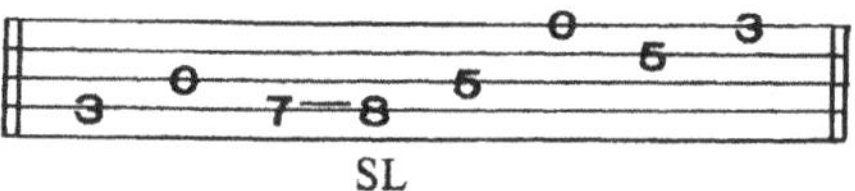

B♭ MAJOR SCALE: This scale can also be used against the G and C chords (blues effect).

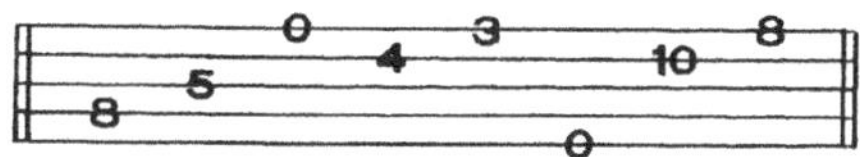

Scales Con't.

CIRCULAR SCALE: A great deal of what is played in the melodic style works along segments of this scale.

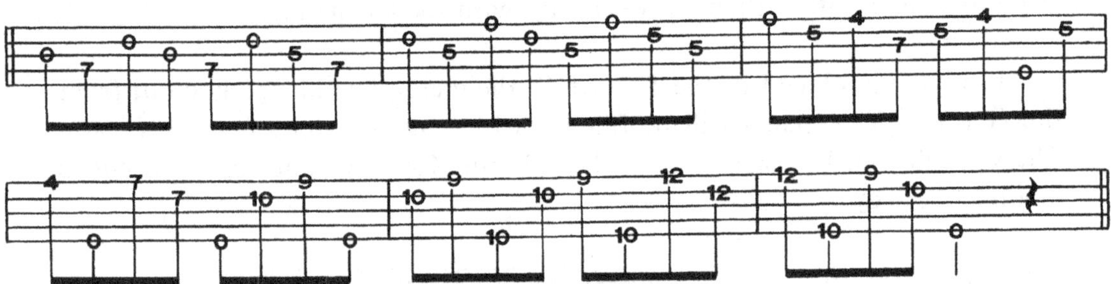

MELODIC LICKS: A lick can be built from the scale belonging to the key of the song or to the chord being applied. Altered tones are also common, (i.e. flat 7th, m 3rd, #5th, etc.)

G CHORD LICKS

C CHORD LICKS

D CHORD LICKS

A & F LICKS

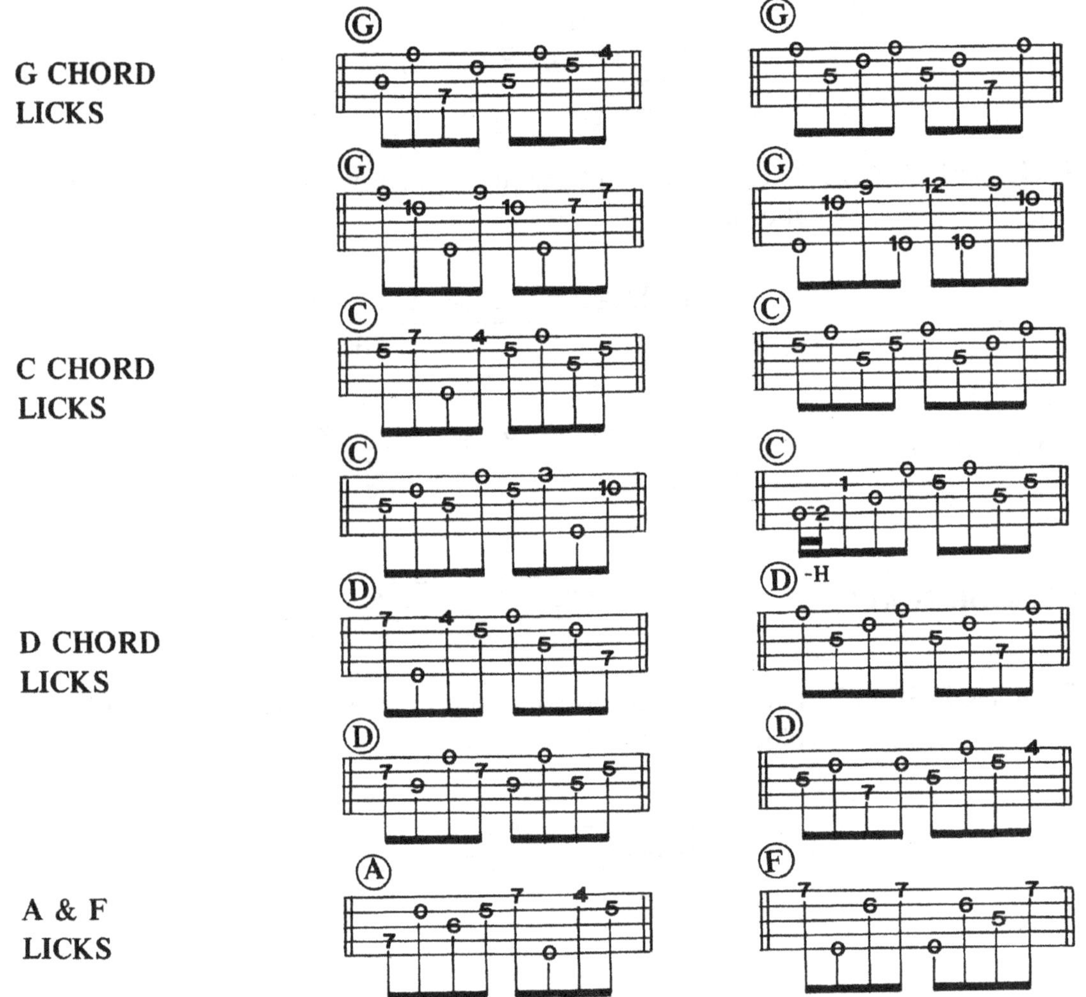

Songs

MELODIC STYLE

CRIPPLE CREEK
Capo 2nd fret to play in the key of A

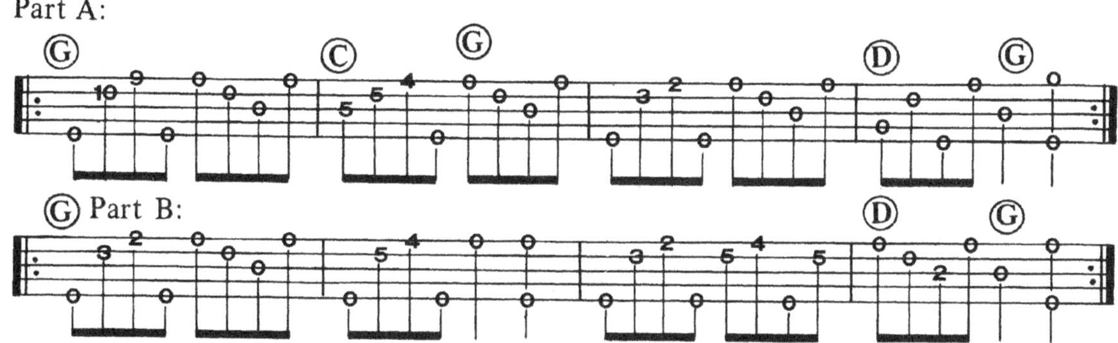

BLACKBERRY BLOSSOM
Key of G

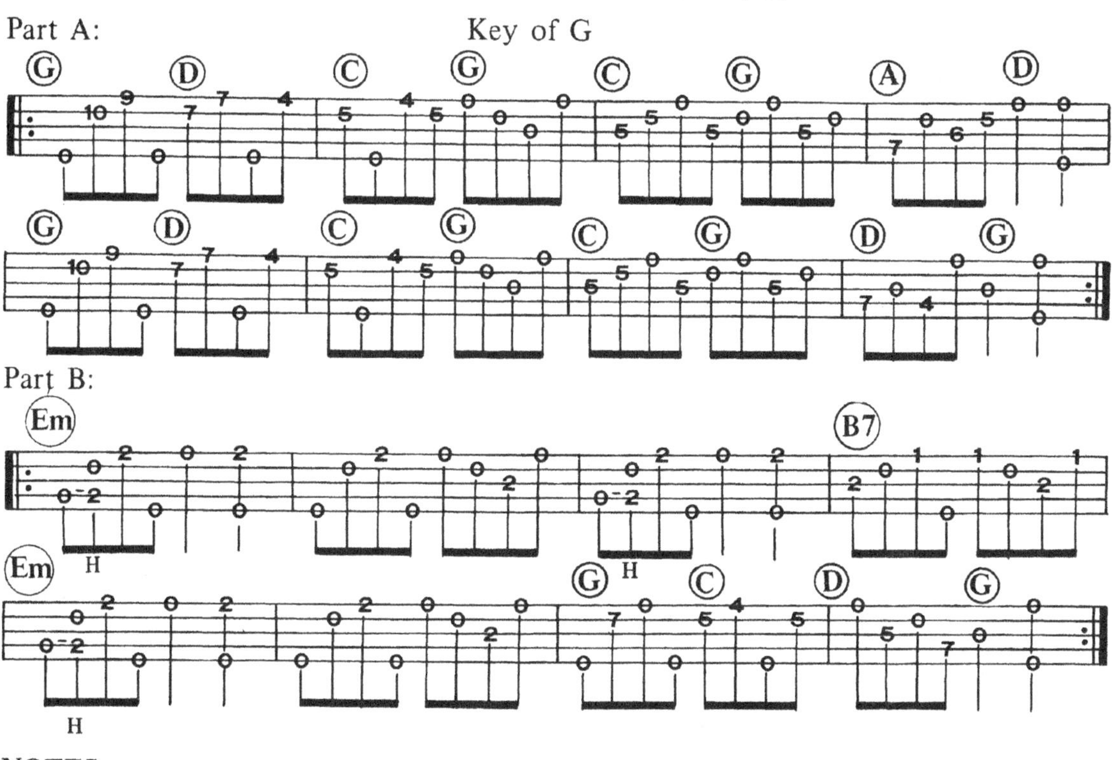

NOTES:

1.) Many of the songs which are played on the banjo in Melodic Style are fiddle tunes which are usually played by fiddle players.

2.) Each fiddle tune is played in a certain key by fiddle players.

3.) Banjo players often use the capo in order to play in these keys: i.e. Key of G= no capo; Key of A=capo 2nd; Key of B♭=capo 3rd, etc. (see p. 75)

FIRE ON THE MOUNTAIN
Capo on the 2nd fret to play in the key A

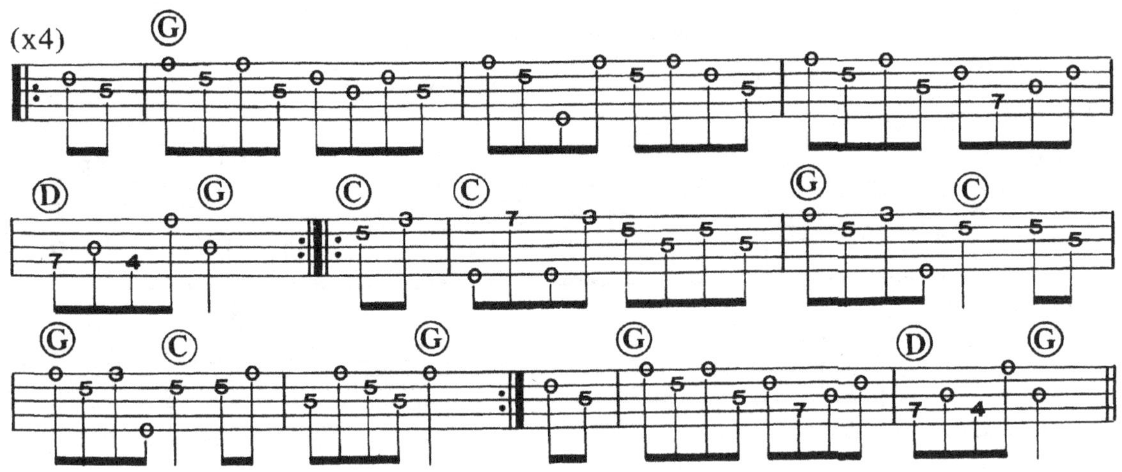

RED HAIRED BOY
To play in the key of A, place the capo on the 2nd fret

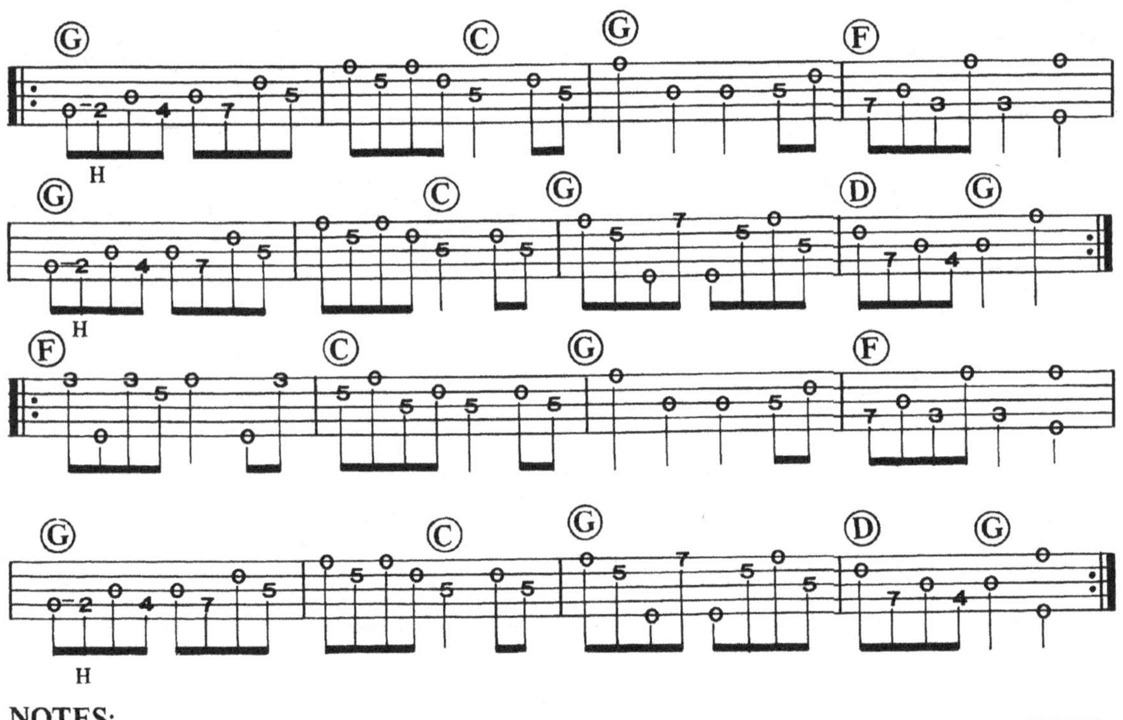

NOTES: ____

1.) Fiddle tunes are usually divided into two sections: Parts A & B.

2.) Each section of a fiddle tune is usually repeated.

THE DUSTY MILLER
Capo 2nd fret for key of A

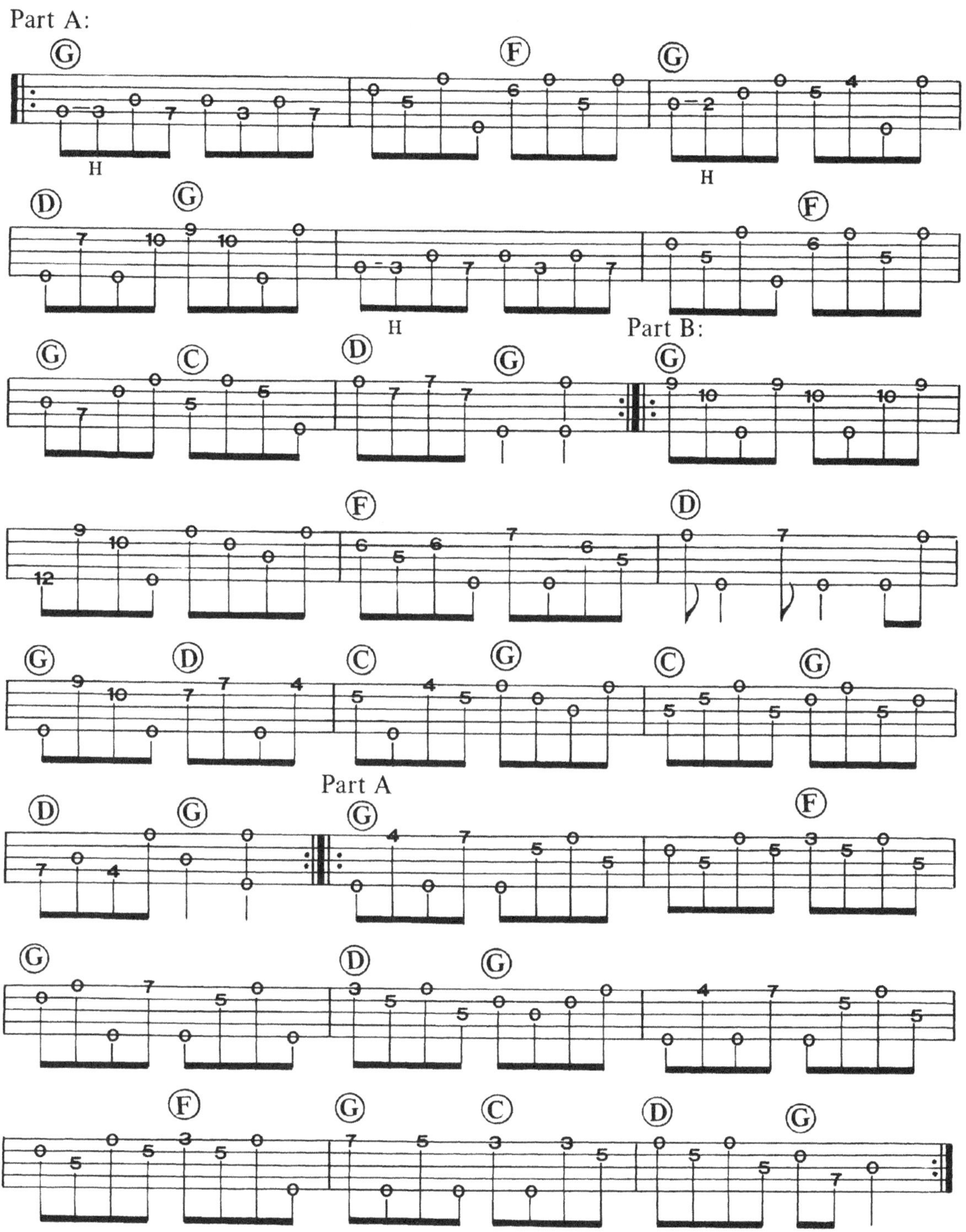

Back Up

BACK UP is another word for accompaniment. When playing with a band, another instrument, or when singing, a banjo player normally plays back up at least 75% of the time.

IN THIS SECTION:

General Guidelines

Vamping Patterns

Back Up Licks

Songs

NOTES:____

1.) For additional information on back up, refer to the book, <u>BACK UP BANJO</u> by Janet Davis, a Mel Bay Publication, (238 pages).

General Guidelines

The back up instruments provide support for the instrument playing or singing the melody.

GENERAL **RULES:**	1.) Don't play as loudly as the lead. 2.) Fill in the spaces. 3.) Try to avoid playing the melody. 4.) Listen to what everyone else is playing and try to work with what they are doing. 5.) Good taste and solid timing are the keys to good back up.
CHORDS & **RHYTHM:**	Back up essentially involves playing a combination of CHORDS and RHYTHM. The left hand works from chord positions, while the right hand plays specific fingering patterns.
PATTERNS:	In addition to the standard rolls and licks which are used to play both lead and back up, there are also patterns which are used primarily for back up only.

NOTES:____

1.) The patterns used for back up can be played for any chord.
2.) These patterns can be used to back almost any song.

Vamping Patterns

Each pattern is a rhythmic pattern which can be played while holding any chord with the left hand. Each pattern should have a percussive effect. To achieve this, dampen, or mute the tones with the left hand by slightly releasing the pressure on the strings.

NOTES:

1.) The same pattern can be played throughout an entire song for each chord in the song, or different patterns can be combined.
2.) Do not press the strings flush against the fingerboard with the left hand; the banjo should "bark".
3.) Vamping patterns usually emphasize beats 2 and 4.

Back Up Licks

The following patterns are used primarily in back up. Each pattern can be played for any chord, but normally works from only one position of each chord, ("F", "D", or "Barre").

COMMON PATTERNS:

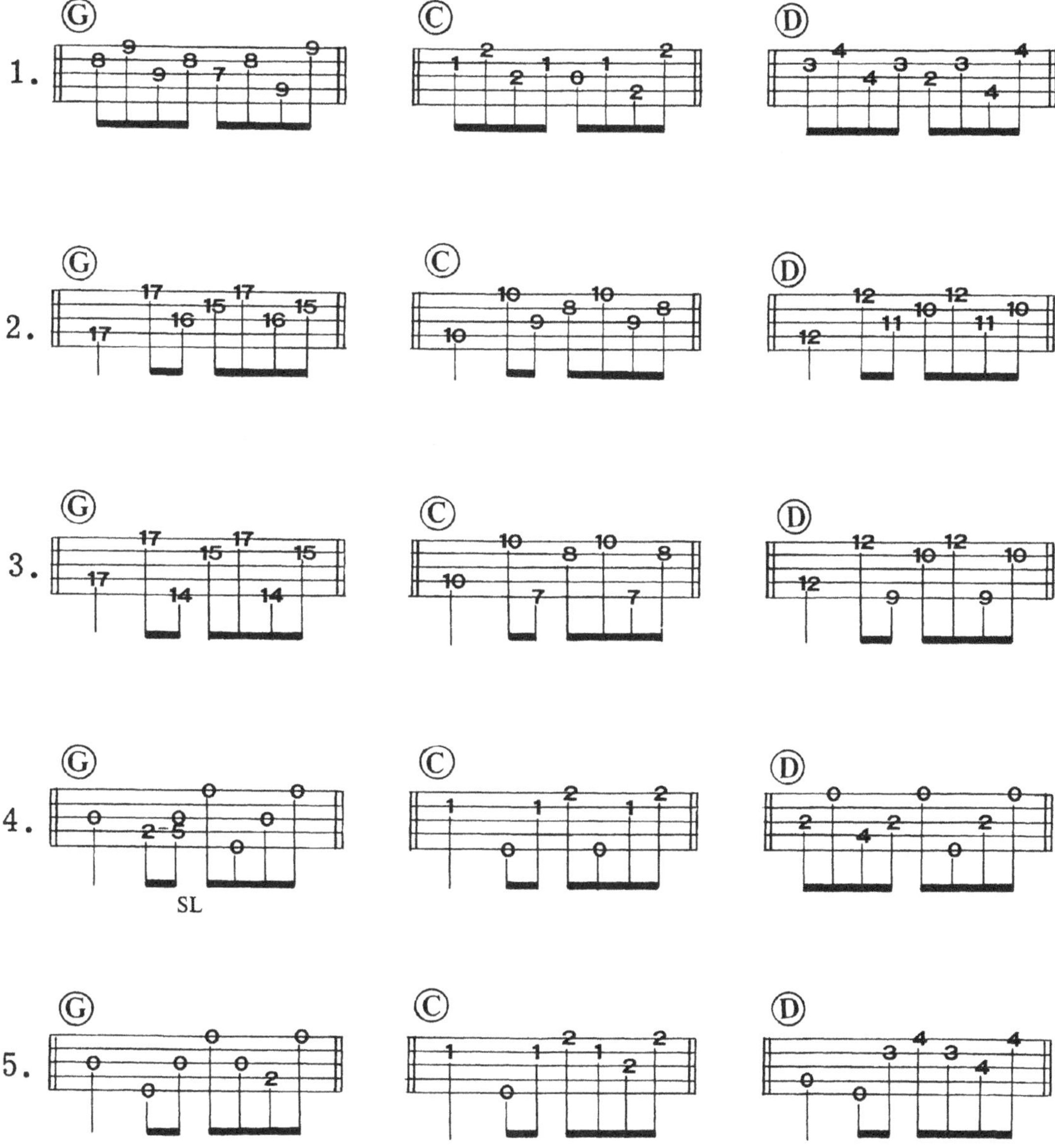

Back Up Licks Con't.

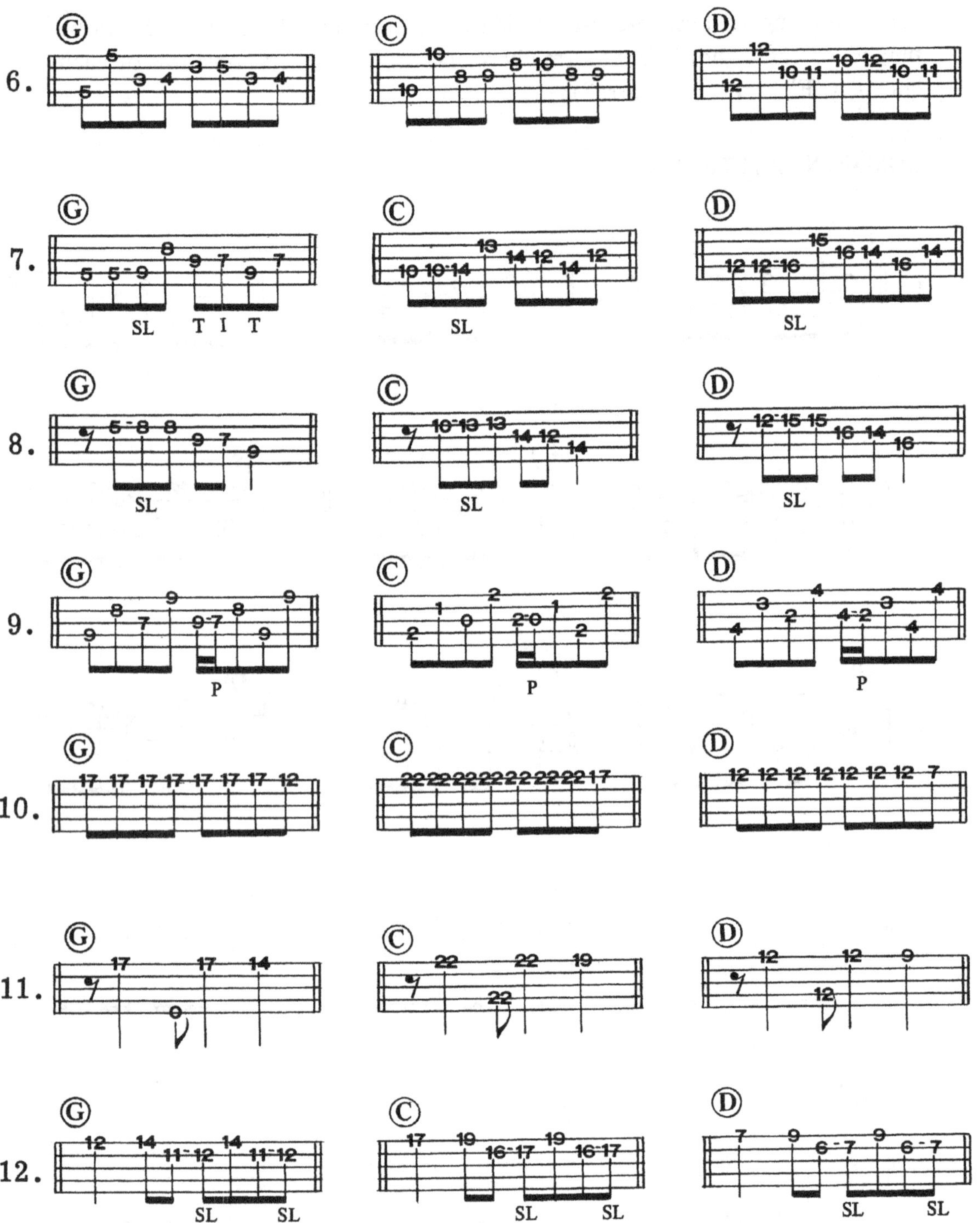

BACK UP LICKS CON'T.

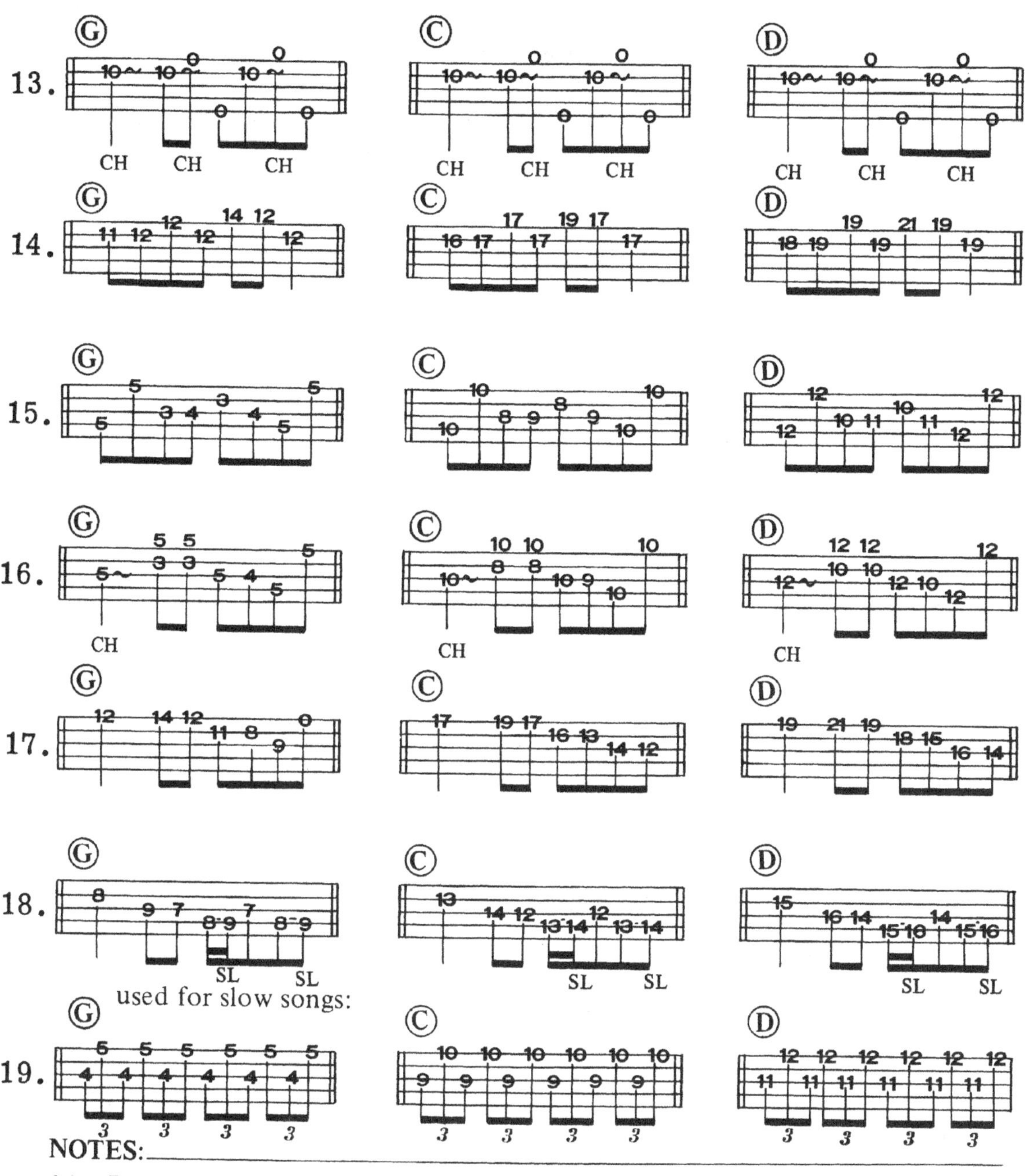

NOTES:

1.) Remember, also, that you can play an entire back up arrangement using only the Standard Roll Patterns.

2.) Also, any lick used to play lead may also be used for backup.

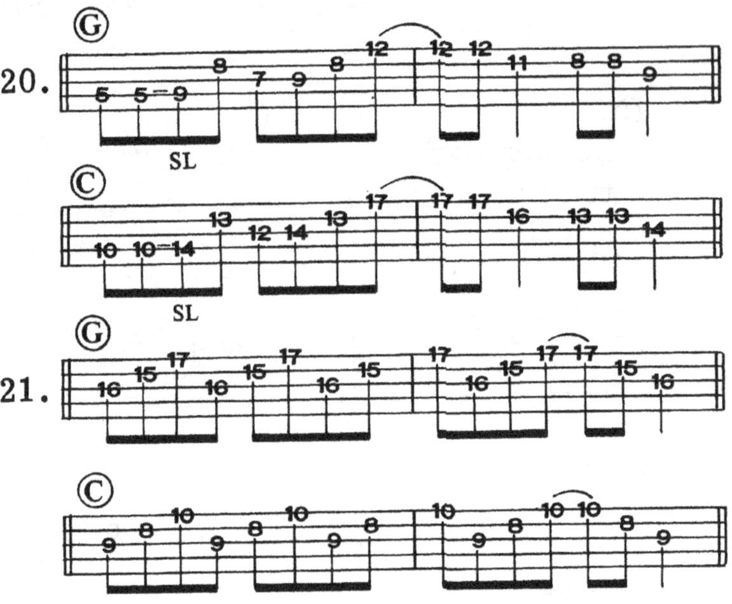

NOTES:

1.) Any two of the above patterns can be combined.

2.) For a useful 2 - measure lick, combine 10 or 11 with 12.

Songs

BACK UP ARRANGEMENTS

Songs consist of various chord progressions, (sequence of certain chords). The same back up patterns can be used for many different songs. Also, you can substitute different patterns as back up for the same song, as long as the patterns apply to the same chords.

BILE EM CABBAGE DOWN
Back Up Using The Basic Vamping Pattern

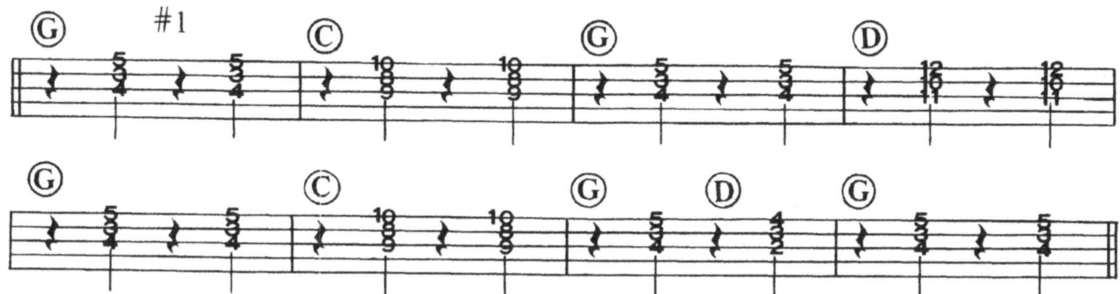

BILE EM CABBAGE DOWN
Back Up Using Standard Back Up Licks

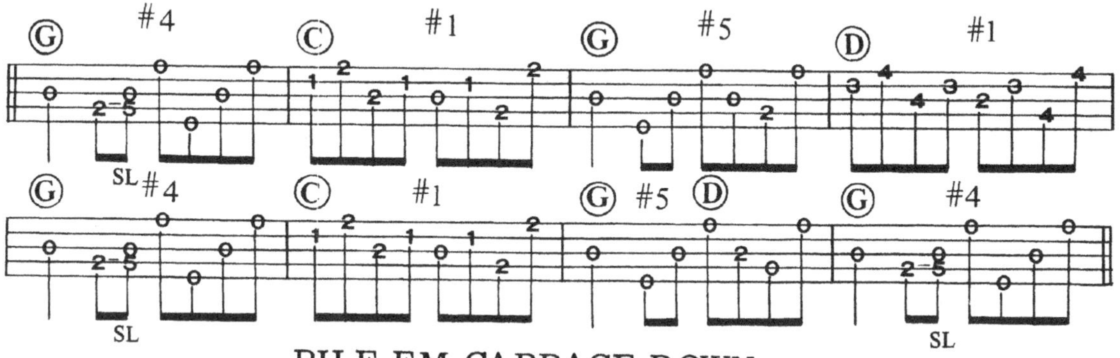

BILE EM CABBAGE DOWN
Using Different Standard Licks

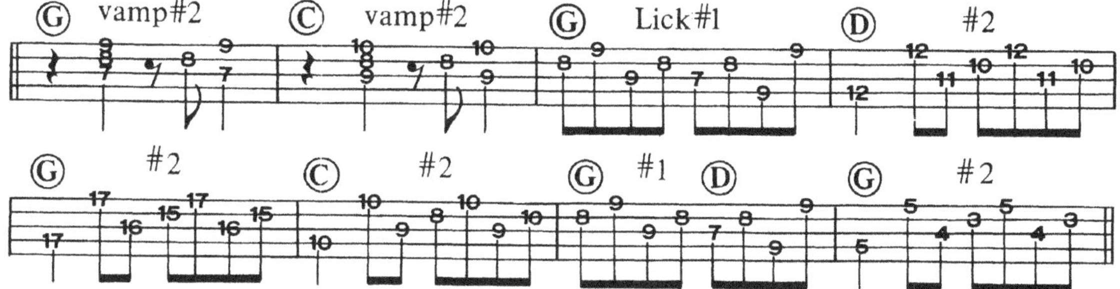

May I Sleep In Your Barn Tonight Mister?
Back Up Arrangement Using Licks #21, #1, & #2

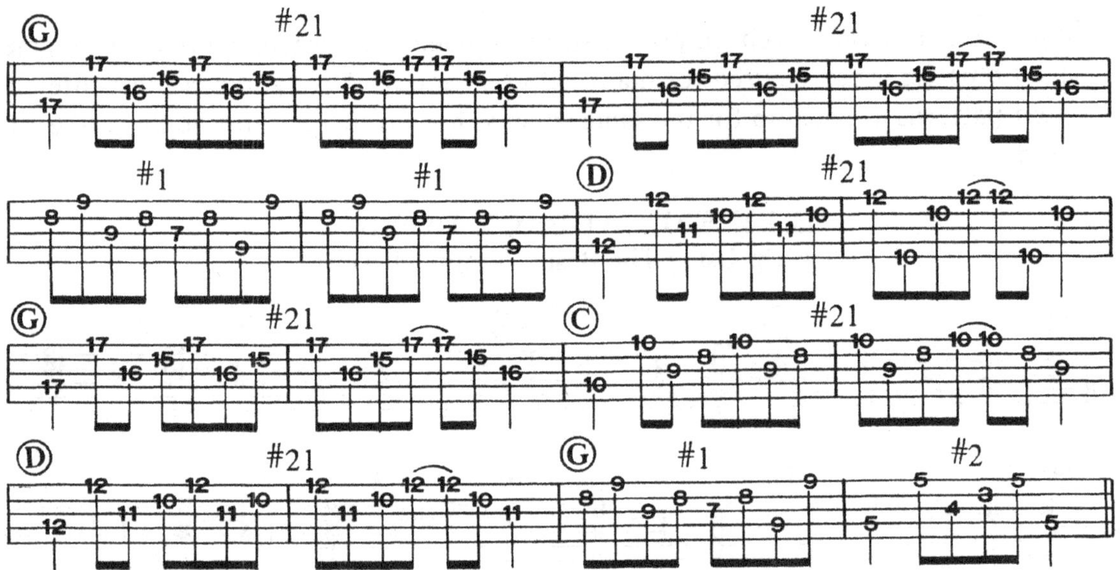

She'll Be Coming Around The Mountain
Back Up Arrangement Using #1, #6, #2

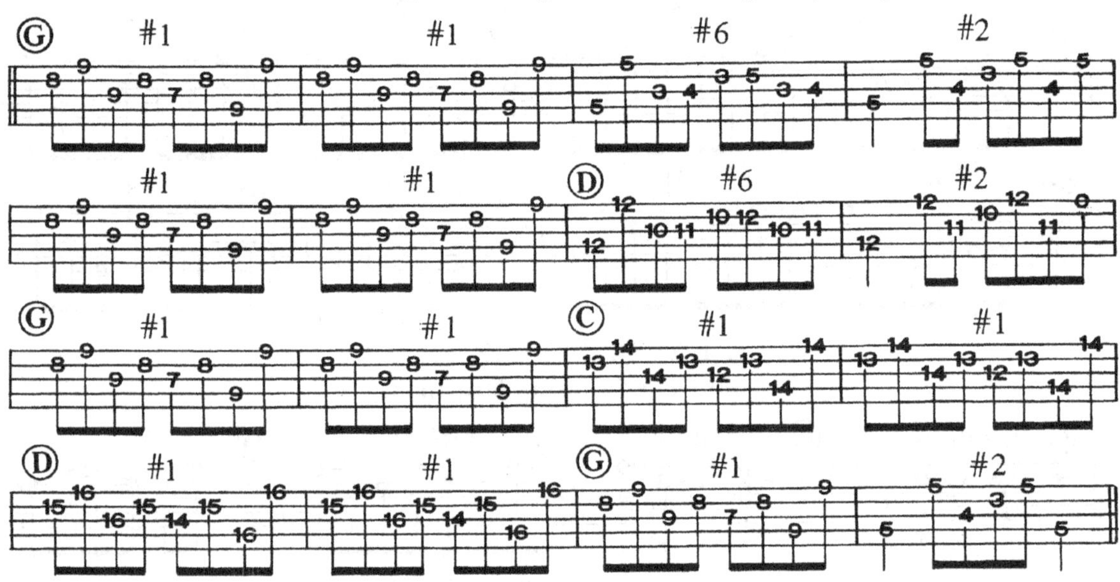

NOTES: ________________________________

1.) Substitute #2 for #6 from the backup licks, (for the same chord).
2.) Notice that both of the above songs use identical chord progressions.
The backup arrangements may be interchanged.

Mama Don't Allow
Back Up Arrangement Using Assorted Licks

Notice that this song uses the same basic chord progression used to back "She'll Be Coming Around The Mountain", and "May I Sleep In Your Barn Tonight, Mister?". Each of these arrangements can be interchanged as back up for the other.

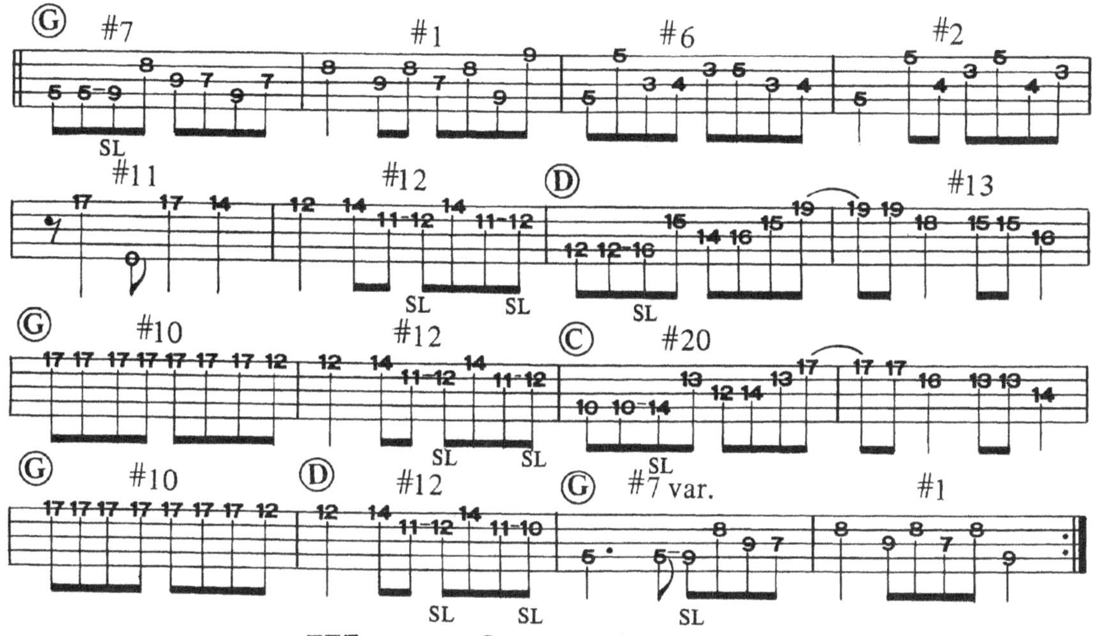

Wreck Of The Old 97
Back Up Arrangement Using Licks #1, #4, & #5

The lick played just before the C chord is also a commonly used lick for this purpose.

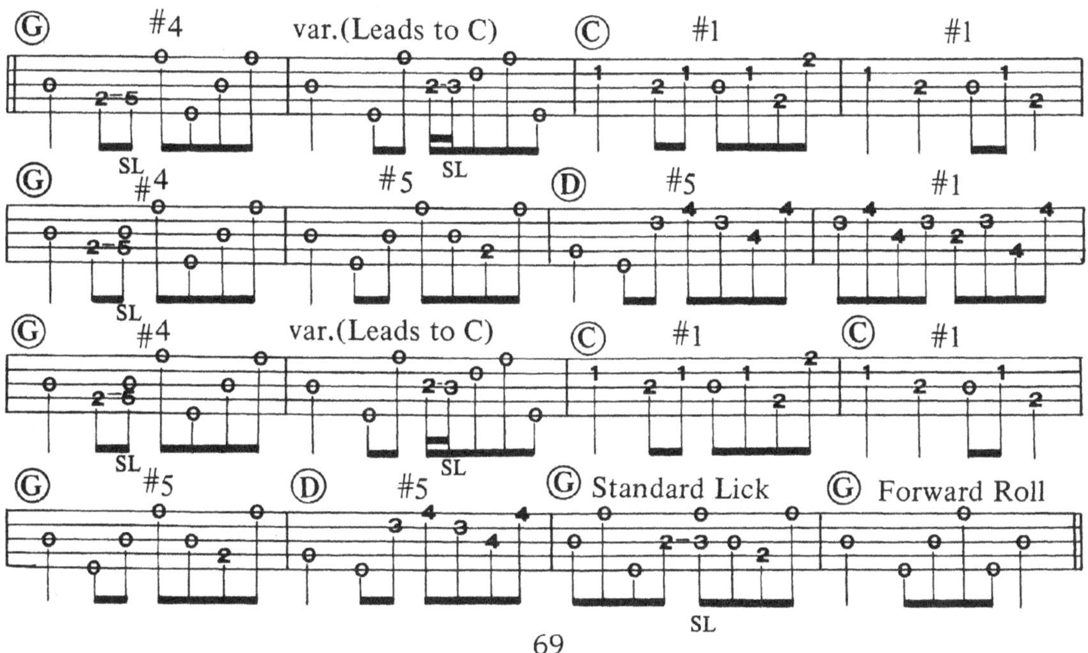

Song Endings

You can combine any Part A with any Part B from the examples below, and tack the combination on to the last two measures of a song, to produce an effective ending, ("tag ending")

OR, you can simply substitute the examples for Part B, for the final two measures of a song. (In other words, the Part B would follow the D chord licks at the close of the song.)

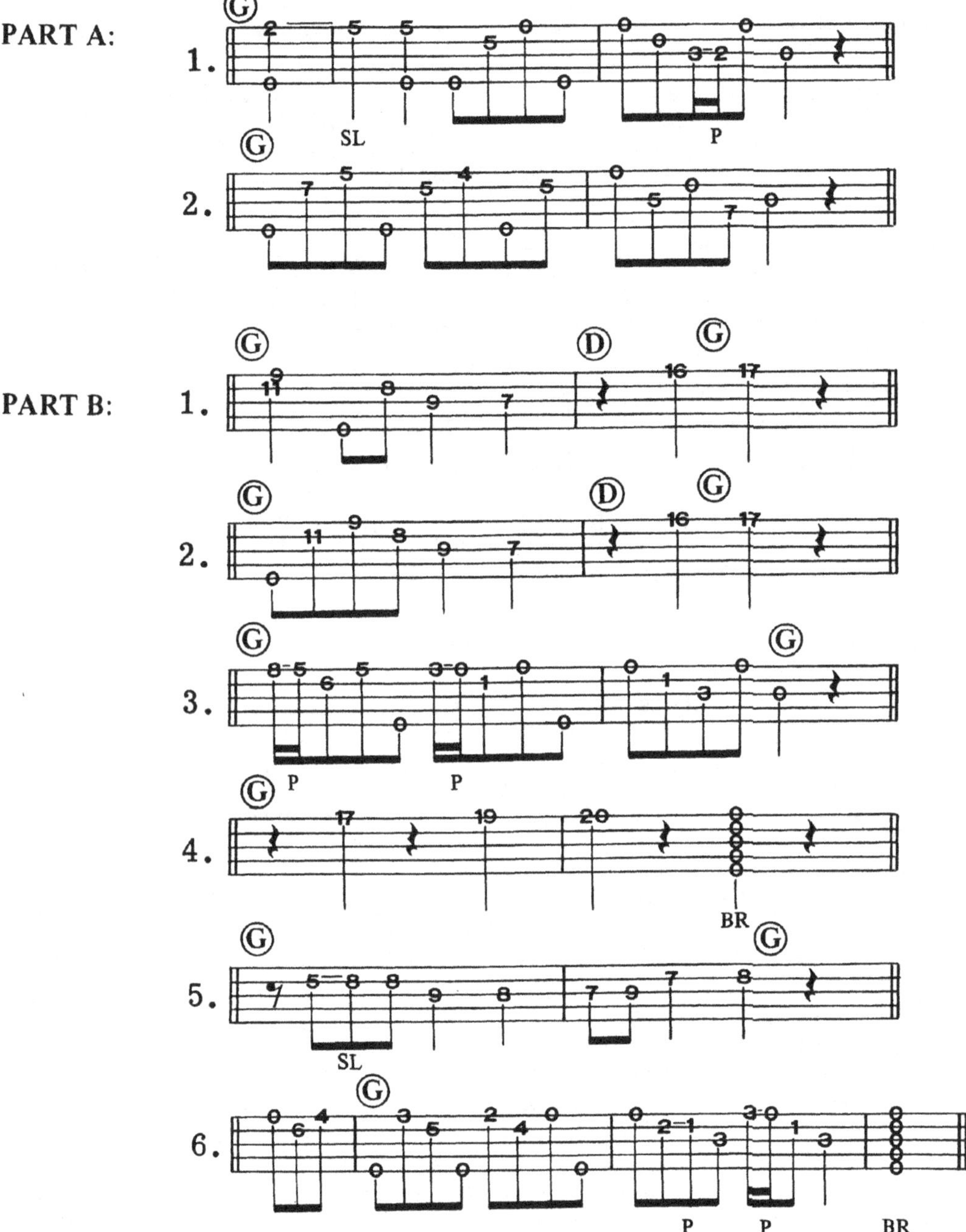

Playing In Any Key

Although many songs are played easily on the banjo in the Key of G, (due to the many possibilities using open strings), any song can be played in any key.

The following sections will discuss the basic methods for playing in keys other than the Key of G.

IN THIS SECTION:

Without Retuning

Using The Capo

Special Tunings
    C Tuning
    D Tuning

Using "D" Tuners

Play In Any Key
WITHOUT RETUNING

The "key" is the tonal center of a song. The same song can be played in any key, but different chords will be used, depending upon the key in which the song is played.

CHORDS: Each "key" uses its own set of specific chords. These chords are built from the scale named for the key, and each chord uses only tones from this scale.

Each chord is numbered. This way, you can transpose a song from one key to another, i.e. play the I chord for the I chord.

Key of G: G Am Bm C D Em F#° G
$\quad$I$\quad$II$\quad$III$\quad$IV V$\quad$VI$\quad$VII I

Key of C: C Dm Em F G Am B° C
$\quad$I$\quad$II$\quad$III$\quad$IV V$\quad$VI$\quad$VII I

LICKS: To play in any key, you simply play rolls and licks for those chords. (Most songs will use the I, IV, and V chords as their basis.)

NOTES:
1.) Because the chords for a "key" use only tones from the specific scale for that key, the I, IV, & V CHORDS will be major chords, and the II, III, and VI are minor chords. The VII chord will always be diminished for any key.
2.) See the following page for examples played in the Key of C, without having to change the tuning of the banjo. Also, see "Just Because" (Key of C), and "Fisher's Hornpipe" (Key of D).

JUST BECAUSE
G Tuning - key of C

This tune is played in the Key of C without retuning the banjo. Basically, this means that the song will use licks for the C, F, and G chords, which are the primary chords used for the Key of C.

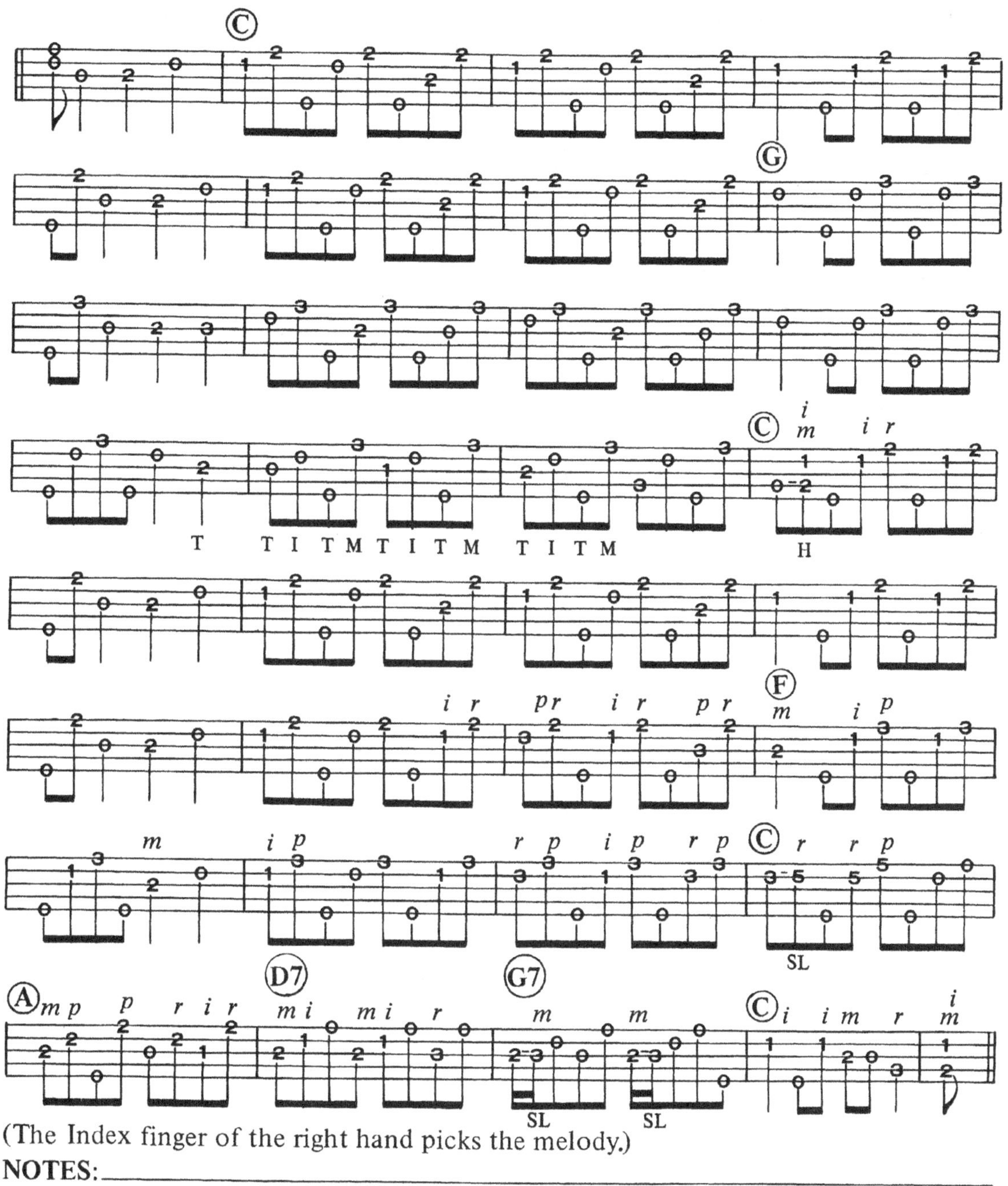

(The Index finger of the right hand picks the melody.)

NOTES:

1. Place the capo on the 2nd fret to play this tune in the Key of D.

FISHER'S HORNPIPE

Key of G

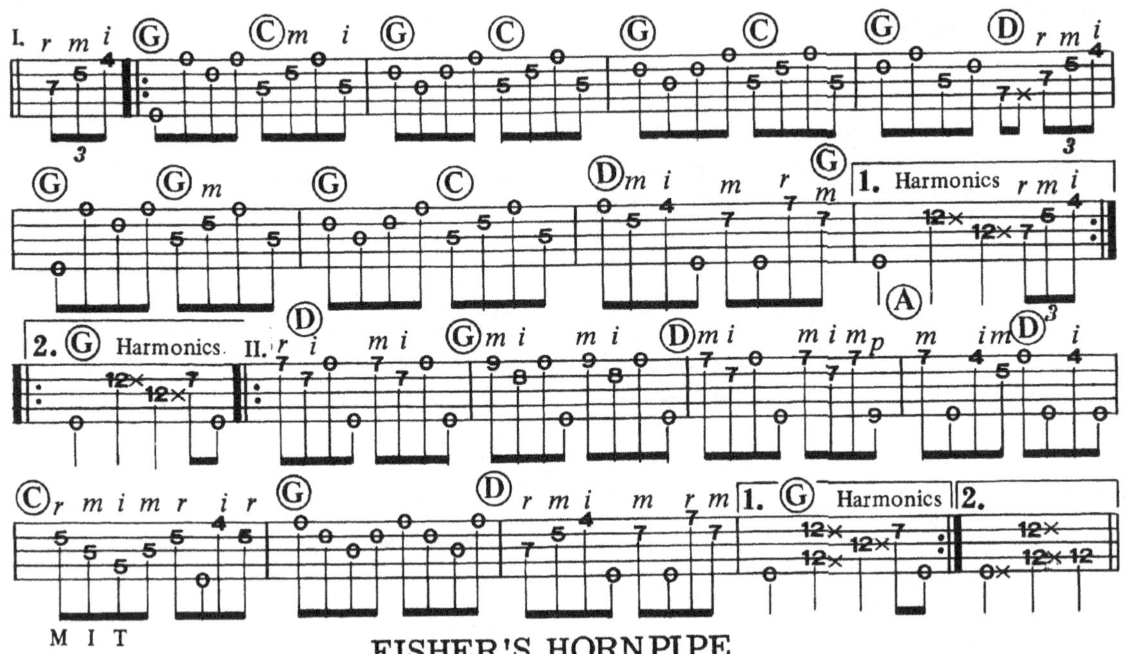

FISHER'S HORNPIPE

This arrangement is played in the Key of D.
It does not, however, call for the capo.
The following is arranged using the D Scale.

Key of D

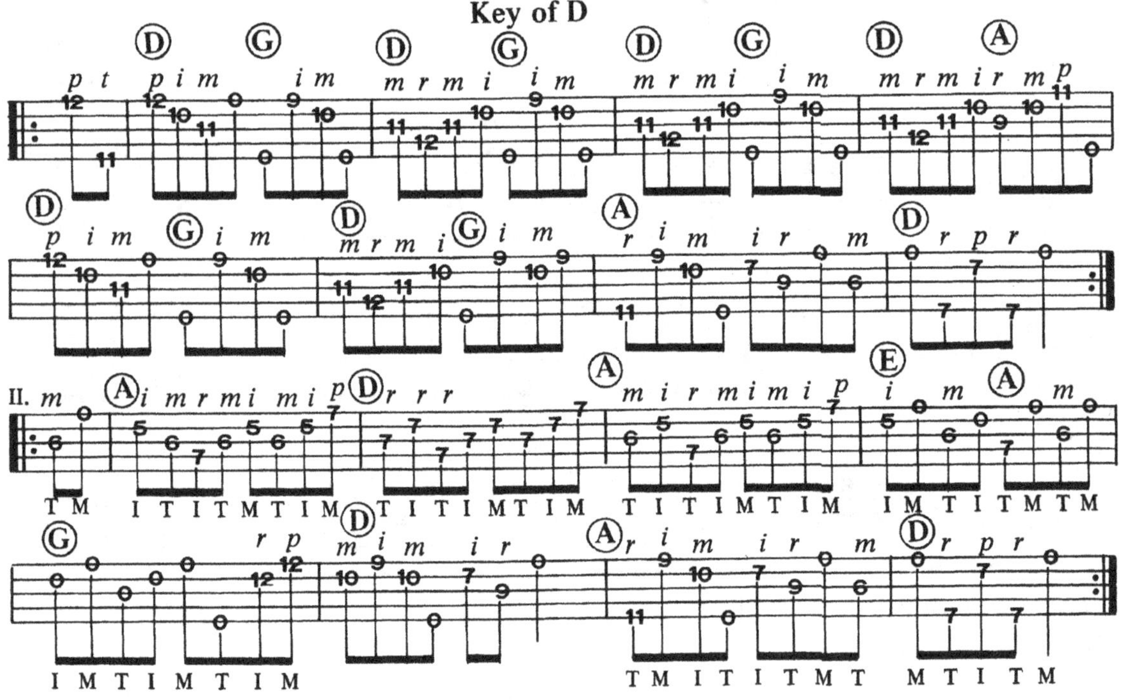

The Capo

Fiddlers and mandolinists, as well as vocalists frequently play each song only in one specific key. To enable the banjo player to play in any key, he can use a capo.

FUNCTION: The capo raises the pitch of the banjo, so that it sounds in a different key.

HOW: A capo can be placed across the strings between two fret bars, to raise the pitch of the banjo. You will play the song from the point of the capo, exactly as you would play from the nut of the banjo. The capo becomes the point of reference.

The 5th string must also be capoed the same distance from the 5th string nut.

TYPES: An elastic (Dunlop) capo, or a clip-on capo, (Shubb or Kyser) are the most popular.

For the 5th string, you can use a sliding capo, (either spring loaded, or the Shubb (screw) 5th string capo), or mini railroad spikes, usually placed on the 2nd, 4th, 5th, & 7th frets of the 5th string.

NOTES:

1.) Some people use a capo simply because they like the sound of the higher pitched banjo for a certain song, rather than for the practical reasons stated above.

Placing The Capo

If playing a song in the Key of G without a capo:

OPEN	(no capo)	= Key of G
Capo	1st fret	= Key of G♯ (A♭)
	2nd fret	= Key of A (common)
	3rd fret	= Key of A♯ (B♭) (common)
	4th fret	= Key of B (common)
	5th fret	= Key of C (common)
	6th fret	= Key of C♯ (D♭)
	7th fret	= Key of D (common)

If playing a song in the Key of C without a capo: (using the C, F, G chords as primary chords)

OPEN	(no capo)	= Key of C
Capo	1st fret	= Key of C♯ (D♭)
	2nd fret	= Key of D (common)
	3rd fret	= Key of D♯ (E♭)
	4th fret	= Key of E (common)
	5th fret	= Key of F (common)
	6th fret	= Key of F♯ (G♭)
	7th fret	= Key of G

NOTES:

1.) Cripple Creek, Red Haired Boy, & Fire On The Mountain are played in the Key of A, (capo 2nd fret); Wreck of the Old 97 is often played in the Key of D, (capo 7th fret).

2.) Relate the capo to the barre position chords: A = 2nd fret; B = 4th fret; C = 5th fret, etc.

3.) Play the banjo as if the capo is the nut. Play the song exactly as you would without the capo, but use the capo as the nut.

Special Tunings

A common method for playing in both the Key of C and also for the Key of D, is to alter the tuning of one or more strings of the banjo.

C TUNING:
G C G B D

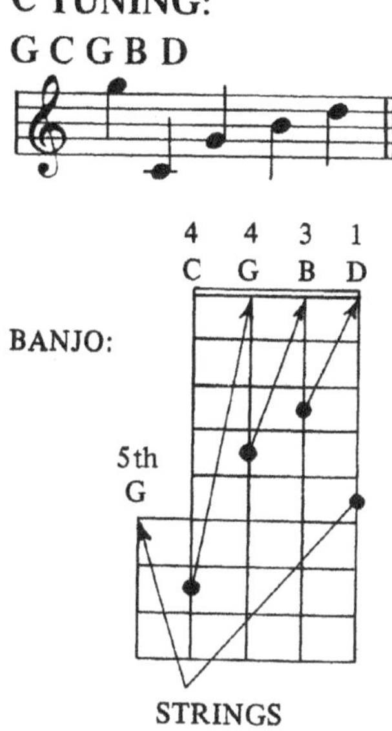

Involves tuning the 4th string of the banjo to a C. (Only this string is altered from the standard G tuning.) This enables the banjo to put a bottom on the C chord, by playing the open 4th string. (See next page). Songs in this tuning use the C, F, & G chords.

1.) Lower the 4th string the equivalent of two frets, to a C tone.

2.) The 4th string at the 7th fret should sound like the open 3rd string.

PIANO:

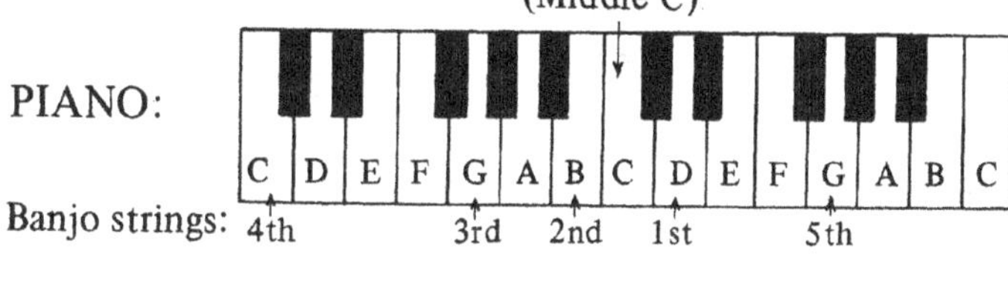

D TUNING:
F D F A D

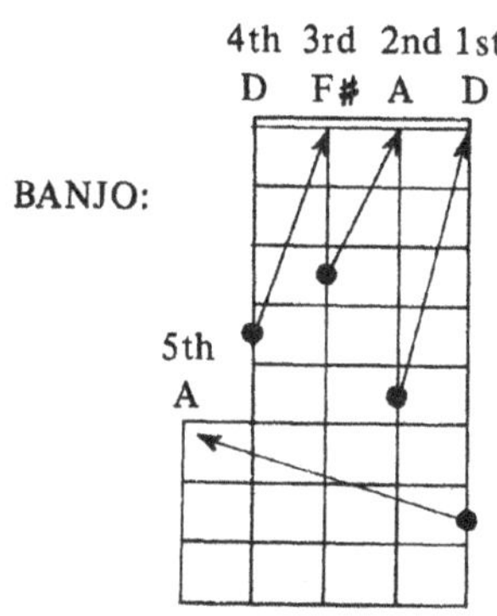

Involves tuning the 2nd string to an A, and the 3rd string to an F#. The 5th string can be tuned to either F# or A. (The 1st and 4th strings are not altered). Notice that the result is a D chord when the strings are played in the open position. (Begin with standard G tuning!)

1.) Lower the 3rd string until it sounds like the 4th string on the 4th fret.

2.) Lower the 2nd string until it sounds like the 4th string on the 7th fret.

3.) Lower the 5th string until it sounds like the 1st string on the 4th fret; or: raise the 5th string to sound like the 1st string at the 7th fret.

PIANO:

Songs

SOLDIER'S JOY
C Tuning

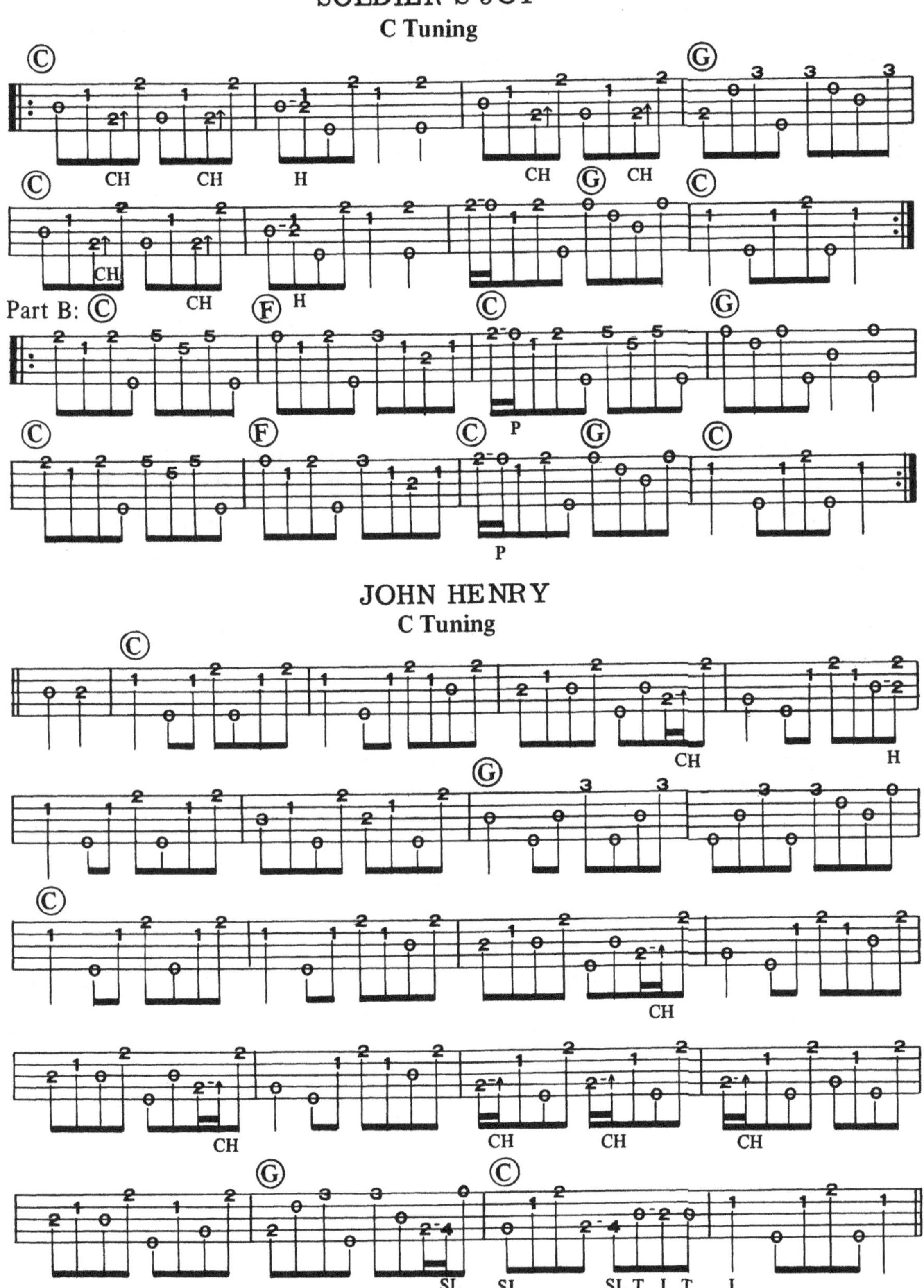

JOHN HENRY
C Tuning

REUBEN
D Tuning

Tune 5th string to F♯, (sounds like 1st string at 4th fret.)

BILE EM CABBAGE
D Tuning

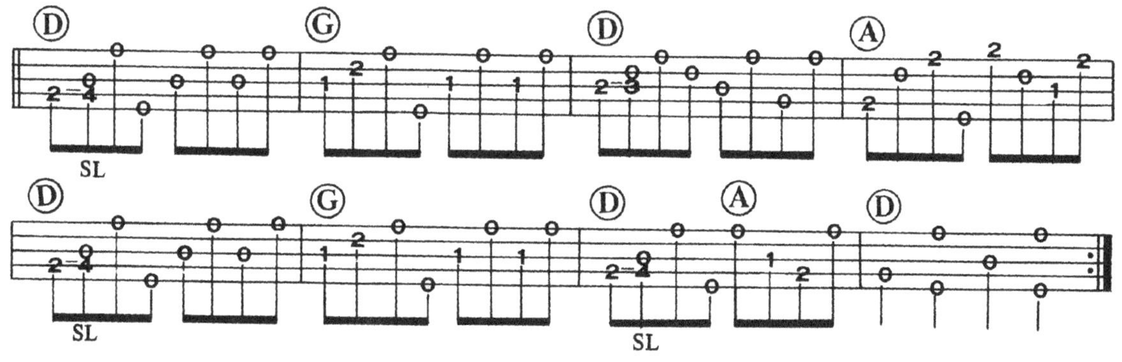

"D" Tuners

"D" Tuners are special tuning pegs which are used in place of the 2nd and 3rd string pegs of your banjo, (and the 1st and 4th if desired).

Each tuner has two stops or screws. The black screw, when tightened, keeps the string from being tuned any higher in pitch; the silver screw keeps the string from being tuned any lower.

The peg will turn only to the point where the screw was tightened, . up or down.

PURPOSE
1.) Tuners can be used to quickly put the banjo in a different tuning, i.e. from G to D tuning.
2.) or they can be used to create a special effect in a song, by turning the pegs up (↑) or down (↓), during the song.

TO SET The usual way to set "D" tuners is:
1.) Tune the banjo to standard G tuning.
Tighten the black buttons.
2.) Tune the banjo to D tuning;
Tighten the silver buttons.

Bile Em Cabbage
Using "D" Tuners

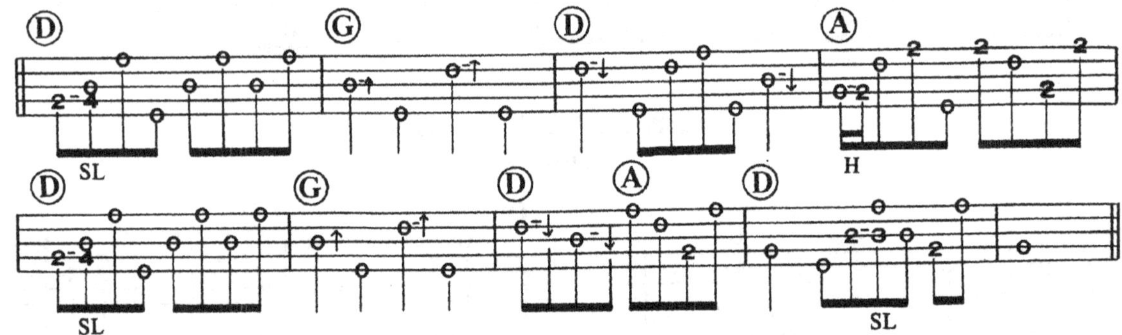

NOTES:
1.) Earl's Breakdown & Flint Hill Special are recorded examples of tuners.
2.) There are many possible settings for tuners, in addition to the above.
3.) Some people use "D" tuners on all 4 strings, (easy to go to C tuning).

Made in the USA
Monee, IL
07 July 2026